Chocolate & Baking

Quick and Easy, Proven Recipes

FLAME TREE
PUBLISHING

Contents

Contents

Chocolate **134**

Contents

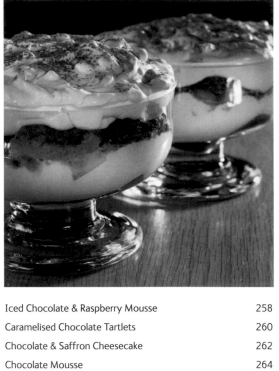

Hygiene in the Kitchen

It is well worth remembering that many foods can carry some form of bacteria. In most cases, the worst it will lead to is a bout of food poisoning or gastroenteritis, although for certain groups this can be more serious. The risk can be reduced or eliminated by good food hygiene and proper cooking.

Do not buy food that is past its sell-by date and do not consume any food that is past its use-by date. When buying food, use the eyes and nose. If the food looks tired, limp or a bad colour or it has a rank, acrid or simply bad smell, do not buy or eat it under any circumstances.

Regularly clean, defrost and clear out the refrigerator or freezer – it is worth checking the packaging to see exactly how long each product is safe to freeze.

Dish cloths and tea towels must be washed and changed regularly. Ideally use disposable cloths which should be replaced on a daily basis. More durable cloths should be left

to soak in bleach, then washed in the washing machine on a boil wash.

Always keep your hands, cooking utensils and food preparation surfaces clean and never allow pets to climb on to any work surfaces.

Buying

Avoid bulk buying where possible, especially fresh produce such as meat, poultry, fish, fruit and vegetables unless buying for the freezer. Fresh foods lose their nutritional value rapidly so buying a little at a time minimises loss of nutrients. It also eliminates a packed refrigerator which reduces the effectiveness of the refrigeration process.

When buying frozen foods, ensure that they are not heavily iced on the outside. Place in the freezer as soon as possible after purchase.

Preparation

Make sure that all work surfaces and utensils are clean and dry. Separate chopping boards should be used for raw and cooked meats, fish and vegetables. It is worth washing all fruits and vegetables regardless of whether they are going to be eaten raw or lightly cooked. Do not reheat food more than once.

All poultry must be thoroughly thawed before cooking. Leave the food in the refrigerator until it is completely thawed. Once defrosted, the chicken should be cooked as soon as possible. The only time food can be refrozen is when the food has been thoroughly thawed then cooked. Once the food has cooled then it can be frozen again for one month.

All poultry and game (except for duck) must be cooked

thoroughly. When cooked the juices will run clear. Other meats, like minced meat and pork should be cooked right the way through. Fish should turn opaque, be firm in texture and break easily into large flakes.

Storing, Refrigerating and Freezing

Meat, poultry, fish, seafood and dairy products should all be refrigerated. The temperature of the refrigerator should be between 1–5°C/34–41°F while the freezer temperature should not rise above -18°C/-0.4°F. When refrigerating cooked food, allow it to cool down quickly and completely before refrigerating. Hot food will raise the temperature of the refrigerator and possibly affect or spoil other food stored in it.

Food within the refrigerator and freezer should always be covered. Raw and cooked food should be stored in separate parts of the refrigerator. Cooked food should be kept on the top shelves of the refrigerator, while raw meat, poultry and fish should be placed on bottom shelves to avoid drips and cross-contamination.

High-Risk Foods

Certain foods may carry risks to people who are considered vulnerable such as the elderly, the ill, pregnant women, babies and those suffering from a recurring illness. It is advisable to avoid those foods which belong to a higher-risk category.

There is a slight chance that some eggs carry the bacteria salmonella. Cook the eggs until both the yolk and the white are firm to eliminate this risk. Sauces including Hollandaise, mayonnaise, mousses, soufflés and meringues all use raw or lightly cooked eggs, as do custard-based dishes, ice creams and sorbets. These are all considered high-risk foods to the vulnerable groups mentioned above. Certain meats and poultry also carry the potential risk of salmonella and so should be cooked thoroughly until the juices run clear and there is no pinkness left. Unpasteurised products such as milk, cheese (especially soft cheese), pâté, meat (both raw and cooked) all have the potential risk of listeria and should be avoided.

When buying seafood, buy from a reputable source. Fish should have bright clear eyes, shiny skin and bright pink or red gills. The fish should feel stiff to the touch, with a slight smell of sea air and iodine. The flesh of fish steaks and fillets should be translucent with no signs of discolouration. Avoid any molluscs that are open or do not close when tapped lightly. Univalves such as cockles or winkles should withdraw into their shells when lightly prodded. Squid and octopus should have firm flesh and a pleasant sea smell.

Care is required when freezing seafood. It is imperative to check whether the fish has been frozen before. If it has been, then it should not be frozen again under any circumstances.

Nutrition

The Role of Essential Nutrients

A healthy and well-balanced diet is the body's primary energy source. In children, it constitutes the building blocks for future health as well as providing lots of energy. In adults, it encourages self-healing and regeneration within the body. A well-balanced diet will provide the body with all the essential nutrients it needs. This can be achieved by eating a variety of foods, demonstrated in the pyramid below:

Fats
milk, yogurt
and cheese

Proteins
meat, fish, poultry, eggs,
nuts and pulses

*Fruits and
Vegetables*

Starchy Carbohydrates
cereals, potatoes, bread, rice and pasta

Fats

Fats fall into two categories: saturated and unsaturated fats. It is very important that a healthy balance is achieved within the diet. Fats are an essential part of the diet and a source of energy and provide essential fatty acids and fat soluble vitamins. The right balance of fats should boost the body's immunity to infection and keep muscles, nerves and arteries in good condition. Saturated fats are of animal origin and are hard when stored at room temperature. They can be found in dairy produce, meat, eggs, margarines and hard white cooking fat (lard) as well as in manufactured products such as pies, biscuits and cakes. A high intake of saturated fat over many years has been proven to increase heart disease and high blood cholesterol levels and often leads to weight gain. The aim of a healthy diet is to keep the fat content low in the foods that we eat. Lowering the amount of saturated fat that we consume is very important, but this does not mean that it is good to consume lots of other types of fat.

There are two kinds of unsaturated fats: poly-unsaturated fats and monounsaturated fats. Poly-unsaturated fats include the following oils: safflower oil, soybean oil, corn oil and sesame oil. Within the polyunsaturated group are Omega oils. The Omega-3 oils are of significant interest because they have been found to be particularly beneficial to coronary health and can encourage brain growth and development. Omega-3 oils are derived from oily fish such as salmon, mackerel, herring, pilchards and sardines. It is recommended that we should eat these types of fish at least once a week. However, for those who do not eat fish or who are vegetarians, liver oil supplements are available in most supermarkers and health shops. It is suggested that these supplements should be taken on a daily basis. The most popular oils that are high in monounsaturates are olive oil, sunflower oil and peanut oil. The Mediterranean diet which is based on a diet high in mono-unsaturated fats is recommended for heart health. Also, monounsaturated fats are known to help reduce the levels of LDL (the bad) cholestrol.

Proteins

Composed of amino acids (proteins' building bricks), proteins perform a wide variety of essential functions for the body including supplying energy and building and repairing tissues. Good sources of proteins are eggs, milk, yogurt, cheese, meat, fish, poultry, eggs, nuts and pulses. (See the second level of the pyramid.) Some of these foods, however, contain saturated fats. To strike a nutritional balance eat generous amounts of vegetable protein foods such as soya, beans, lentils, peas and nuts.

Fruits and Vegetables

Not only are fruits and vegetables the most visually appealing foods, but they are extremely good for us, providing essential vitamins and minerals essential for growth, repair and protection in the human body. Fruits and vegetables are low in calories and

are responsible for regulating the body's metabolic processes and controlling the composition of its fluids and cells.

Minerals

CALCIUM Important for healthy bones and teeth, nerve transmission, muscle contraction, blood clotting and hormone function. Calcium promotes a healthy heart, improves skin, relieves aching muscles and bones, maintains the correct acid-alkaline balance and reduces menstrual cramps. Good sources are dairy products, small bones of small fish, nuts, pulses, fortified white flours, breads and green leafy vegetables.

CHROMIUM Part of the glucose tolerance factor, chromium balances blood sugar levels, helps to normalise hunger and reduce cravings, improves lifespan, helps protect DNA and is essential for heart function. Good sources are brewer's yeast, wholemeal bread, rye bread, oysters, potatoes, green peppers, butter and parsnips.

IODINE Important for the manufacture of thyroid hormones and for normal development. Good sources of iodine are seafood, seaweed, milk and dairy products.

IRON As a component of haemoglobin, iron carries oxygen around the body. It is vital for normal growth and development. Good sources are liver, corned beef, red meat, fortified breakfast cereals, pulses, green leafy vegetables, egg yolk and cocoa and cocoa products.

MAGNESIUM Important for efficient functioning of metabolic enzymes and development of the skeleton. Magnesium promotes healthy muscles by helping them to relax and is therefore good for PMS. It is also important for heart muscles and the nervous system. Good sources are nuts, green vegetables, meat, cereals, milk and yogurt.

PHOSPHORUS Forms and maintains bones and teeth, builds muscle tissue, helps maintain pH of the body aids metabolism and energy production. Phosphorus is present in almost all foods.

POTASSIUM Enables nutrients to move into cells, while waste products move out; promotes healthy nerves and muscles; maintains fluid balance in the body; helps secretion of insulin for blood sugar control to produce constant energy; relaxes muscles; maintains heart functioning and stimulates gut movement to encourage proper elimination. Good sources are fruit, vegetables, milk and bread.

SELENIUM Antioxidant properties help to protect against free radicals and carcinogens. Selenium reduces inflammation, stimulates the immune system to fight infections, promotes a healthy heart and helps vitamin E's action. It is also required for the male reproductive system and is needed for metabolism. Good sources are tuna, liver, kidney, meat, eggs, cereals, nuts and dairy products.

SODIUM Important in helping to control body fluid and balance, preventing dehydration. Sodium is involved in muscle and nerve function and helps move nutrients into cells. All foods are good sources, however processed, pickled and salted foods are richest in sodium.

ZINC Important for metabolism and the healing of wounds. It also aids ability to cope with stress, promotes a healthy

nervous system and brain especially in the growing foetus, aids bones and teeth formation and is essential for constant energy. Good sources are liver, meat, pulses, whole-grain cereals, nuts and oysters.

Vitamins

VITAMIN A Important for cell growth and developmemt and for the formation of visual pigments in the eye. Vitamin A comes in two forms: retinol and beta-carotenes. Retinol is found in liver, meat and meat products and whole milk and its products. Beta-carotene is a powerul antioxidant and is found in red and yellow fruits and vegetables such as carrots, mangoes and apricots.

VITAMIN B1 Important in releasing energy from carboydrate-containing foods. Good sources are yeast and yeast products, bread, fortified breakfast cereals and potatoes.

VITAMIN B2 Important for metabolism of proteins, fats and carbohydrates to produce energy. Good sources are meat, yeast extracts, fortified breakfast cereals and milk and its products.

VITAMIN B3 Required for the metabolism of food into energy production. Good sources are milk and milk products, fortified breakfast cereals, pulses, meat, poultry and eggs.

VITAMIN B5 Important for the metabolism of food and energy production. All foods are good sources but especially fortified breakfast cereals, whole-grain bread and dairy products.

VITAMIN B6 Important for metabolism of protein and fat. Vitamin B6 may also be involved with the regulation of sex hormones. Good sources are liver, fish, pork, soya beans and peanuts.

VITAMIN B12 Important for the production of red blood cells and DNA. It is vital for growth and the nervous system. Good sources are meat, fish, eggs, poultry and milk.

BIOTIN Important for metabolism of fatty acids. Good sources of biotin are liver, kidney, eggs and nuts. Micro-organisms also manufacture this vitamin in the gut.

VITAMIN C Important for healing wounds and the formation of collagen which keeps skin and bones strong. It is an important antioxidant. Good sources are fruits, soft summer fruits and vegetables.

VITAMIN D Important for absorption and handling of calcium to help build bone strength. Good sources are oily fish, eggs, whole milk and milk products, margarine and of course sufficient exposure to sunlight, as vitamin D is made in the skin.

VITAMIN E Important as an antioxidant vitamin helping to protect cell membranes from damage. Good sources are vegetable oils, margarines, seeds, nuts and green vegetables.

FOLIC ACID Critical during pregnancy for the development of the brain and nerves. It is always essential for brain and nerve function and is needed for utilising protein and red blood cell formation. Good sources are whole-grain cereals, fortified breakfast cereals, green leafy vegetables, oranges and liver.

VITAMIN K Important for controlling blood clotting. Good sources are cauliflower, Brussels sprouts, lettuce, cabbage, beans, broccoli, peas, asparagus, potatoes, corn oil, tomatoes and milk.

Carbohydrates

Carbohydrates are an energy source and come in two forms: starch and sugar carbohydrates. Starch carbohydrates are also known as complex carbohydrates and they include all cereals, potatoes, breads, rice and pasta. (See the fourth level of the pyramid). Eating whole-grain varieties of these foods also provides fibre. Diets high in fibre are believed to be beneficial in helping to prevent bowel cancer and can also keep cholesterol down. High-fibre diets are also good for those concerned about weight gain. Fibre is bulky so fills the stomach, therefore reducing hunger pangs. Sugar carbohydrates which are also known as fast-release carbohydrates (because of the quick fix of energy they give to the body) include sugar and sugar-sweetened products such as jams and syrups. Milk provides lactose which is a milk sugar and fruits provide fructose which is a fruit sugar.

Baking

Ginger Snaps

MAKES 40

300 g/11 oz butter or
  margarine, softened
225 g/8 oz soft light
  brown sugar
75 g/3 oz black treacle

1 medium egg
400 g/14 oz plain flour
2 tsp bicarbonate of soda
½ tsp salt
1 tsp ground ginger

1 tsp ground cloves
1 tsp ground cinnamon
50 g/2 oz granulated sugar

Preheat the oven to 190°C/375°F/Gas Mark 5, 10 minutes before baking. Lightly oil a baking sheet.

Cream together the butter or margarine and the sugar until light and fluffy.

Warm the treacle in the microwave for 30–40 seconds, then add gradually to the butter mixture with the egg. Beat until combined well.

In a separate bowl, sift the flour, bicarbonate of soda, salt, ground ginger, ground cloves and ground cinnamon. Add to the butter mixture and mix together to form a firm dough.

Chill in the refrigerator for 1 hour. Shape the dough into small balls and roll in the granulated sugar. Place well apart on the oiled baking sheet.

Sprinkle the baking sheet with a little water and transfer to the preheated oven.

Bake for 12 minutes, until golden and crisp. Transfer to a wire rack to cool and serve.

Try this: FOR AN ALTERNATIVE: 64   FOR KIDS: 32

Spiced Palmier Biscuits with Apple Purée

MAKES 20

250 g/9 oz prepared puff
    pastry, thawed if frozen
40 g/1½ oz caster sugar
25 g/1 oz icing sugar
1 tsp ground cinnamon

¼ tsp ground ginger
¼ tsp freshly grated nutmeg
450 g/1 lb Bramley cooking
    apples, roughly chopped
50 g/2 oz sugar

25 g/1 oz raisins
25 g/1 oz dried cherries
zest of 1 orange
double cream, lightly
    whipped, to serve

Preheat the oven to 200°C/400°F/Gas Mark 6, 15 minutes before baking. Roll out the pastry on a lightly floured surface to form a 25.5 x 30.5 cm/10 x 12 inch rectangle. Trim the edges with a small sharp knife.

Sift together the caster sugar, icing sugar, cinnamon, ginger and nutmeg into a bowl. Generously dust both sides of the pastry sheet with about a quarter of the sugar mixture. With a long edge facing the body, fold either side halfway towards the centre. Dust with a third of the remaining sugar mixture. Fold each side again so that they almost meet in the centre and dust again with about half the remaining sugar mixture. Fold the two sides together down the centre of the pastry to give six layers altogether. Wrap the pastry in clingfilm and refrigerate for 1–2 hours until firm. Reserve the remaining spiced sugar.

Remove the pastry from the refrigerator, unwrap and roll in the remaining sugar to give a good coating all round. Using a sharp knife, cut the roll into about 20 thin slices. Place the cut side down on to a baking sheet and place in the pre-heated oven. Cook for 10 minutes, turn the biscuits over and cook for a further 5–10 minutes, or until golden and crisp. Remove from the oven and transfer to a wire rack. Allow to cool completely.

Meanwhile, combine the remaining ingredients in a saucepan. Cover and cook gently for 15 minutes until the apple is completely soft. Stir well and allow to cool. Serve the palmiers with a spoonful of the apple purée and a little of the whipped double cream

Try this: FOR AN ALTERNATIVE: 46   FOR KIDS: 34

Whipped Shortbread

MAKES 36

225 g/8 oz butter, softened
75 g/3 oz icing sugar
175 g/6 oz plain flour

hundreds and thousands
sugar strands
chocolate drops

silver balls
50 g/2 oz icing sugar
2–3 tsp lemon juice

Preheat the oven to 180°C/350°F/Gas Mark 4, 10 minutes before baking. Lightly oil a baking sheet.

Cream the butter and icing sugar until fluffy. Gradually add the flour and continue beating for a further 2–3 minutes until it is smooth and light.

Roll into balls and place on a baking sheet. Cover half of the dough mixture with hundreds and thousands, sugar strands, chocolate drops or silver balls. Keep the other half plain.

Bake in the preheated oven for 6–8 minutes, until the bottoms are lightly browned. Remove from the oven and transfer to a wire rack to cool.

Sift the icing sugar into a small bowl. Add the lemon juice and blend until a smooth icing forms.

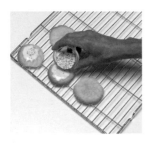

Using a small spoon, swirl the icing over the cooled plain cookies. Decorate with either the extra hundreds and thousands, chocolate drops or silver balls and serve.

Try this: FOR AN ALTERNATIVE: 178   FOR KIDS: 138

Jammy Buns

MAKES 12

175 g/6 oz plain flour
175 g/6 oz wholemeal flour
2 tsp baking powder
150 g/5 oz butter

or margarine
125 g/4 oz golden
caster sugar
50 g/2 oz dried cranberries

1 large egg, beaten
1 tbsp milk
4–5 tbsp seedless
raspberry jam

Preheat the oven to 190°C/375°F/Gas Mark 5, 10 minutes before baking. Lightly oil a large baking sheet.

Sift the flours and baking powder together into a large bowl, then tip in the grains remaining in the sieve.

Cut the butter or margarine into small pieces. It is easier to do this when the butter is in the flour as it helps stop the butter from sticking to the knife.

Rub the butter into the flours until it resembles coarse breadcrumbs. Stir in the sugar and cranberries.

Using a round bladed knife stir in the beaten egg and milk. Mix to form a firm dough. Divide the mixture into 12 and roll into balls.

Place the dough balls on the baking tray, leaving enough space for expansion. Press your thumb into the centre of each ball to make a small hollow. Spoon a little of the jam in each hollow. Pinch lightly to seal the tops.

Bake in the preheated oven for 20–25 minutes, or until golden brown. Cool on a wire rack and serve.

 Try this: FOR AN ALTERNATIVE: 106   FOR KIDS: 176

Cappuccino Cakes

MAKES 6

125 g/4 oz butter or margarine
125 g/4 oz caster sugar
2 medium eggs

1 tbsp strong black coffee
150 g/5 oz self-raising flour
125 g/4 oz mascarpone cheese

1 tbsp icing sugar, sifted
1 tsp vanilla essence
sifted cocoa powder, to dust

Preheat the oven to 190°C/375°F/Gas Mark 5, 10 minutes before baking. Place six large paper muffin cases into a muffin tin or alternatively place on to a baking sheet.

Cream the butter or margarine and sugar together until light and fluffy. Break the eggs into a small bowl and beat lightly with a fork. Using a wooden spoon, beat the eggs into the butter and sugar mixture a little at a time, until they are all incorporated.

If the mixture looks curdled beat in a spoonful of the flour to return the mixture to a smooth consistency. Finally beat in the black coffee.

Sift the flour into the mixture, then with a metal spoon or rubber spatula gently fold in the flour. Place spoonfuls of the mixture into the muffin cases.

Bake in the preheated oven for 20–25 minutes, or until risen and springy to the touch. Cool on a wire rack.

In a small bowl beat together the mascarpone cheese, icing sugar and vanilla essence. When the cakes are cold, spoon the vanilla mascarpone on to the top of each one. Dust with cocoa powder and serve. Eat within 24 hours and store in the refrigerator.

Try this: FOR AN ALTERNATIVE: 56   FOR KIDS: 182

Coconut & Almond Munchies

MAKES 26-30

5 medium egg whites
250 g/9 oz icing sugar, plus
   extra to sprinkle

225 g/8 oz ground almonds
200 g/7 oz desiccated coconut
grated rind of 1 lemon

125 g/4 oz milk chocolate
125 g/4 oz white chocolate

Preheat the oven to 150°C/300°F/Gas Mark 2, 10 minutes before baking. Line several baking sheets with rice paper. Place the egg whites in a clean, grease-free bowl and whisk until stiff and standing in peaks. Sift the icing sugar, then carefully fold half of the sugar into the whisked egg whites together with the ground almonds. Add the coconut, the remaining icing sugar and the lemon rind and mix together to form a very sticky dough.

Place the mixture in a piping bag and pipe the mixture into walnut-sized mounds onto the rice paper, then sprinkle with a little extra icing sugar. Bake in the preheated oven for 20–25 minutes, or until set and golden on the outside. Remove from the oven and leave to cool slightly. Using a spatula, carefully transfer to a wire rack and leave until cold.

Break the milk and white chocolate into pieces and place in two separate bowls. Melt both chocolates set over saucepans of gently simmering water. Alternatively, melt in the microwave, according to the manufacturer's instructions. Stir until smooth and free from lumps. Dip one edge of each munchie in the milk chocolate and leave to dry on non-stick baking parchment. When dry, dip the other side into the white chocolate. Leave to set, then serve as soon as possible.

Try this: FOR AN ALTERNATIVE: 30 FOR KIDS: 22

Almond Macaroons

MAKES 12

rice paper	1 tsp ground rice	8 blanched almonds,
125 g/4 oz caster sugar	2–3 drops almond essence	halved
50 g/2 oz ground almonds	1 medium egg white	

Preheat the oven to 150°C/300°F/Gas Mark 2, 10 minutes before baking. Line a baking sheet with the rice paper.

Mix the caster sugar, ground almonds, ground rice and almond essence together and reserve.

Whisk the egg white until stiff then gently fold in the caster sugar mixture with a metal spoon or rubber spatula.

Mix to form a stiff but not sticky paste. If the mixture is very sticky, add a little extra ground almonds. Place small spoonfuls of the mixture, about the size of an apricot, well apart on the rice paper.

Place a half-blanched almond in the centre of each. Place in the preheated oven and bake for 25 minutes, or until just pale golden.

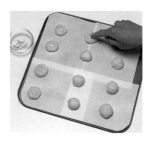

Remove the biscuits from the oven and leave to cool for a few minutes on the baking sheet. Cut or tear the rice paper around the macaroons to release them. Once cold, serve them or store in an airtight tin.

Try this: FOR AN ALTERNATIVE: 140   FOR KIDS: 58

Fruit & Nut Flapjacks

MAKES 12

75 g/3 oz butter or margarine	3 tbsp golden syrup	175 g/6 oz rolled oats
125 g/4 oz soft light brown sugar	50 g/2 oz raisins	50 g/2 oz icing sugar
	50 g/2 oz walnuts, roughly chopped	1–1½ tbsp lemon juice

Preheat the oven to 180°C/350°F/Gas Mark 4, 10 minutes before baking. Lightly oil a 23 cm/9 inch square cake tin.

Melt the butter or margarine with the sugar and syrup in a small saucepan over a low heat. Remove from the heat. Stir the raisins, walnuts and oats into the syrup mixture and mix together well.

Spoon evenly into the prepared tin and press down well. Transfer to the preheated oven and bake for 20–25 minutes.

Remove from the oven and leave to cool in the tin. Cut into bars while still warm.

Sift the icing sugar into a small bowl then gradually beat in the lemon juice a little at a time to form a thin icing.

Place into an icing bag fitted with a writing nozzle then pipe thin lines over the flapjacks. Allow to cool and serve.

Try this: FOR AN ALTERNATIVE: 164 FOR KIDS: 144

Apple & Cinnamon Crumble Bars

MAKES 16

450 g/1 lb Bramley cooking
    apples, roughly chopped
50 g/2 oz raisins
50 g/2 oz caster sugar
1 tsp ground cinnamon

zest of 1 lemon
200 g/7 oz plain flour
250 g/9 oz soft light
    brown sugar
½ tsp bicarbonate of soda

150 g/5 oz rolled oats
150 g/5 oz butter, melted
crème fraîche or whipped
    cream, to serve

Preheat the oven to 190°C/375°F/Gas Mark 5, 10 minutes before baking. Place the apples, raisins, sugar, cinnamon and lemon zest into a saucepan over a low heat.

Cover and cook for about 15 minutes, stirring occasionally, until the apple is cooked through. Remove the cover and stir well with a wooden spoon to break up the apple completely.

Cook for a further 15–30 minutes over a very low heat until reduced, thickened and slightly darkened. Allow to cool. Lightly oil and line a 20.5 cm/8 inch square cake tin with greaseproof or baking paper.

Mix together the flour, sugar, bicarbonate of soda, rolled oats and butter until combined well and crumbly. Spread half of the flour mixture into the bottom of the prepared tin and press down. Pour over the apple mixture.

Sprinkle over the remaining flour mixture and press down lightly. Bake in the preheated oven for 30–35 minutes, until golden brown.

Remove from the oven and allow to cool before cutting into slices. Serve the bars warm or cold with crème fraîche or whipped cream.

Try this: FOR AN ALTERNATIVE: 20   FOR KIDS: 48

Lemon Bars

MAKES 24

175 g/6 oz flour
125 g/4 oz butter
50 g/2 oz granulated sugar
200 g/7 oz caster sugar

2 tbsp flour
½ tsp baking powder
¼ tsp salt
2 medium eggs,

lightly beaten
juice and finely grated
rind of 1 lemon
sifted icing sugar, to decorate

Preheat the oven to 170°C/325°F/Gas Mark 3, 10 minutes before baking. Lightly oil and line a 20.5 cm/8 inch square cake tin with greaseproof or baking paper.

Rub together the flour and butter until the mixture resembles breadcrumbs. Stir in the granulated sugar and mix.

Turn the mixture into the prepared tin and press down firmly. Bake in the preheated oven for 20 minutes, until pale golden.

Meanwhile, in a food processor, mix together the caster sugar, flour, baking powder, salt, eggs, lemon juice and rind until smooth. Pour over the prepared base.

Transfer to the preheated oven and bake for a further 20–25 minutes, until nearly set but still a bit wobbly in the centre. Remove from the oven and cool in the tin on a wire rack.

Dust with icing sugar and cut into squares. Serve cold or store in an airtight tin.

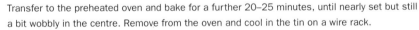

Try this: FOR AN ALTERNATIVE: 72 FOR KIDS: 38

Lemon–iced Ginger Squares

MAKES 12

225 g/8 oz caster sugar
50 g/2 oz butter, melted
2 tbsp black treacle
2 medium egg whites,
    lightly whisked

225 g/8 oz plain flour
1 tsp bicarbonate of soda
½ tsp ground cloves
1 tsp ground cinnamon
¼ tsp ground ginger

pinch of salt
225 ml/8 fl oz buttermilk
175 g/6 oz icing sugar
lemon juice

Preheat the oven to 200°C/400°F/Gas Mark 6, 15 minutes before baking. Lightly oil a 20.5 cm/8 inch square cake tin and sprinkle with a little flour.

Mix together the caster sugar, butter and treacle. Stir in the egg whites.

In a separate bowl, mix together the flour, bicarbonate of soda, cloves, cinnamon, ginger and salt. Stir the flour mixture and buttermilk alternately into the butter mixture until blended well.

Spoon into the prepared tin and bake in the preheated oven for 35 minutes, or until a skewer inserted into the centre of the cake comes out clean.

Remove from the oven and allow to cool for 5 minutes in the tin before turning out on to a wire rack over a large plate. Using a cocktail stick, make holes on the top of the cake.

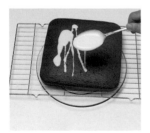

Meanwhile, mix together the icing sugar with enough lemon juice to make a smooth pourable icing. Carefully pour the icing over the hot cake, then leave until cold. Cut the ginger cake into squares and serve.

Try this: FOR AN ALTERNATIVE: 64 FOR KIDS: 142

Maple, Pecan & Lemon Loaf

CUTS TO 12 SLICES

350 g/12 oz plain flour
1 tsp baking powder
175 g/6 oz butter, cubed
75 g/3 oz caster sugar
125 g/4 oz pecan nuts,

roughly chopped
3 medium eggs
1 tbsp milk
finely grated rind of 1 lemon
5 tbsp maple syrup

For the icing:
75 g/3 oz icing sugar
1 tbsp lemon juice
25 g/1 oz pecans,
roughly chopped

Preheat the oven to 170°C/325°F/Gas Mark 3, 10 minutes before baking. Lightly oil and line the base of a 900 g/2 lb loaf tin with non-stick baking parchment.

Sift the flour and baking powder into a large bowl. Rub in the butter until the mixture resembles fine breadcrumbs. Stir in the caster sugar and pecan nuts.

Beat the eggs together with the milk and lemon rind. Stir in the maple syrup. Add to the dry ingredients and gently stir in until mixed thoroughly to make a soft dropping consistency.

Spoon the mixture into the prepared tin and level the top with the back of a spoon. Bake on the middle shelf of the preheated oven for 50–60 minutes, or until the cake is well risen and lightly browned. If a skewer inserted into the centre comes out clean, then the cake is ready.

Leave the cake in the tin for about 10 minutes, then turn out and leave to cool on a wire rack. Carefully remove the lining paper.

Sift the icing sugar into a small bowl and stir in the lemon juice to make a smooth icing.

Drizzle the icing over the top of the loaf, then scatter with the chopped pecans. Leave to set, thickly slice and serve.

Try this: FOR AN ALTERNATIVE: 42 FOR KIDS: 36

Moist Mincemeat Tea Loaf

CUTS INTO 12 SLICES

225 g/8 oz self-raising flour
½ tsp ground mixed spice
125 g/4 oz cold butter, cubed
75 g/3 oz flaked almonds
25 g/1 oz glacé cherries,

rinsed, dried
and quartered
75 g/3 oz light
muscovado sugar
2 medium eggs

250 g/9 oz prepared
mincemeat
1 tsp lemon zest
2 tsp brandy or milk

Preheat the oven to 180°C/350°F/Gas Mark 4, 10 minutes before cooking. Oil and line the base of a 900 g/2 lb loaf tin with non-stick baking paper.

Sift the flour and mixed spice into a large bowl. Add the butter and rub in until the mixture resembles breadcrumbs.

Reserve 2 tablespoons of the flaked almonds and stir in the rest with the glacé cherries and sugar. Make a well in the centre of the dry ingredients. Lightly whisk the eggs, then stir in the mincemeat, lemon zest and brandy or milk.

Add the egg mixture and fold together until blended. Spoon into the prepared loaf tin, smooth the top with the back of a spoon, then sprinkle over the reserved flaked almonds.

Bake on the middle shelf of the preheated oven for 30 minutes. Cover with tinfoil to prevent the almonds browning too much. Bake for a further 30 minutes, or until well risen and a skewer inserted into the centre comes out clean.

Leave the tea loaf in the tin for 10 minutes before removing and cooling on a wire rack. Remove the lining paper, slice thickly and serve.

Try this: FOR AN ALTERNATIVE: 40   FOR KIDS: 180

Citrus Cake

CUTS INTO 8 SLICES

175 g/6 oz golden
caster sugar
175 g/6 oz butter
or margarine
3 medium eggs

2 tbsp orange juice
175 g/6 oz self-raising flour
finely grated rind of
2 oranges
5 tbsp lemon curd

125 g/4 oz icing sugar
finely grated rind of 1 lemon
1 tbsp freshly squeezed
lemon juice

Preheat the oven to 325°C/170°F/Gas Mark 3, 10 minutes before baking. Lightly oil and line the base of a deep, round 20.5 cm/8 inch cake tin with baking paper.

In a large bowl, cream the sugar and butter or margarine together until light and fluffy. Whisk the eggs together and beat into the creamed mixture a little at a time.

Beat in the orange juice with 1 tablespoon of the flour. Sift the remaining flour on to a large plate several times, then with a metal spoon or rubber spatula, fold into the creamed mixture.

Spoon into the prepared cake tin. Stir the finely grated orange rind into the lemon curd and dot randomly across the top of the mixture.

Using a fine skewer swirl the lemon curd through the cake mixture. Bake in the preheated oven for 35 minutes, until risen and golden. Allow to cool for 5 minutes in the tin, then turn out carefully on to a wire rack.

Sift the icing sugar into a bowl, add the grated lemon rind and juice and stir well to mix. When the cake is cold, cover the top with the icing and serve.

Try this: FOR AN ALTERNATIVE: 72   FOR KIDS: 36

Autumn Bramley Apple Cake

CUTS INTO 8-10 SLICES

225 g/8 oz self-raising flour
1½ tsp baking powder
150 g/5 oz margarine, softened
150 g/5 oz caster sugar, plus extra for sprinkling
1 tsp vanilla essence
2 large eggs, beaten
1.1 kg/2½ lbs Bramley cooking apples, peeled, cored and sliced
1 tbsp lemon juice
½ tsp ground cinnamon
fresh custard or cream, to serve

Preheat the oven to 170°C/325°F/Gas Mark 3, 10 minutes before baking. Lightly oil and line the base of a deep 20.5 cm/8 inch cake tin with non-stick baking paper.

Sift the flour and baking powder into a small bowl. Beat the margarine, sugar and vanilla essence until light and fluffy. Gradually beat in the eggs a little at a time, beating well after each addition. Stir in the flour mixture.

Spoon about one-third of the mixture into the tin, smoothing the surface. Toss the apple slices in the lemon juice and cinnamon and spoon over the cake mixture, making a thick, even layer. Spread the remaining mixture over the apple layer to the edge of the tin, making sure the apples are covered. Smooth the top with the back of a wet spoon and sprinkle generously with sugar.

Bake in the preheated oven for 1½ hours, or until well risen and golden, the apples are tender and the centre of the cake springs back when pressed lightly. Reduce the oven temperature slightly and cover the cake loosely with tinfoil if the top browns too quickly.

Transfer to a wire rack and cool for about 20 minutes in the tin. Run a thin knife blade between the cake and the the tin to loosen the cake, and invert on to a paper-lined rack. Turn the cake the right way up and cool. Serve with the custard or cream.

Try this: FOR AN ALTERNATIVE: 34 FOR KIDS: 188

Apple & Cinnamon Crumble–top Cake

CUTS INTO 8 SLICES

For the topping:
350 g/12 oz eating
    apples, peeled
1 tbsp lemon juice
125 g/4 oz self-raising flour
1 tsp ground cinnamon
75 g/3 oz butter or margarine

75 g/3 oz demerara sugar
1 tbsp milk

For the base:
125 g/4 oz butter or margarine
125 g/4 oz caster sugar
2 medium eggs

150 g/5 oz self-raising flour

cream or freshly made
    custard, to serve.

Preheat the oven to 180°C/350°F/Gas Mark 4, 10 minutes before baking. Lightly oil and line the base of a 20.5 cm/8 inch deep round cake tin with greaseproof or baking paper.

Finely chop the apples and mix with the lemon juice. Reserve while making the cake.

For the crumble topping, sift the flour and cinnamon together into a large bowl. Rub the butter or margarine into the flour and cinnamon until the mixture resembles coarse breadcrumbs. Stir the sugar into the mixture and reserve.

For the base, cream the butter or margarine and sugar together until light and fluffy. Gradually beat the eggs into the sugar and butter mixture a little at a time until all the egg has been added. Sift the flour and gently fold in with a metal spoon or rubber spatula.

Spoon into the base of the prepared cake tin. Arrange the apple pieces on top, then lightly stir the milk into the crumble mixture.

Scatter the crumble mixture over the apples and bake in the preheated oven for 1½ hours. Serve cold with cream or custard.

Try this: FOR AN ALTERNATIVE: 34   FOR KIDS: 192

Carrot Cake

CUTS INTO 8 SLICES

200 g/7 oz plain flour
½ tsp ground cinnamon
½ tsp freshly grated nutmeg
1 tsp baking powder
1 tsp bicarbonate of soda
150 g/5 oz dark
   muscovado sugar

200 ml/7 fl oz vegetable oil
3 medium eggs
225 g/8 oz carrots, peeled
   and roughly grated
50 g/2 oz chopped walnuts

For the icing:
175 g/6 oz cream cheese
finely grated rind of
   1 orange
1 tbsp orange juice
1 tsp vanilla essence
125 g/4 oz icing sugar

Preheat the oven to 150°C/300°F/Gas Mark 2, 10 minutes before baking. Lightly oil and line the base of a deep 15 cm/6 inch square cake tin with greaseproof paper.

Sift the flour, spices, baking powder and bicarbonate of soda together into a large bowl. Stir in the dark muscovado sugar and mix together. Lightly whisk the oil and eggs together, then gradually stir into the flour and sugar mixture. Stir well.

Add the carrots and walnuts. Mix thoroughly, then pour into the prepared cake tin. Bake in the preheated oven for 1¼ hours, or until light and springy to the touch and a skewer inserted into the centre of the cake comes out clean.

Remove from the oven and allow to cool in the tin for 5 minutes before turning out on to a wire rack. Reserve until cold.

To make the icing, beat together the cream cheese, orange rind, orange juice and vanilla essence. Sift the icing sugar and stir into the cream cheese mixture.

When cold, discard the lining paper, spread the cream cheese icing over the top and serve cut into squares.

Try this: FOR AN ALTERNATIVE: 68 FOR KIDS: 60

Apricot & Almond Slice

CUTS INTO 10 SLICES

2 tbsp demerara sugar	225 g/8 oz caster sugar	50 g/2 oz ready-to-eat dried
25 g/1 oz flaked almonds	4 medium eggs	apricots, chopped
400 g can apricot	200 g/7 oz self-raising flour	3 tbsp clear honey
halves, drained	25 g/1 oz ground almonds	3 tbsp roughly chopped
225 g/8 oz butter	½ tsp almond essence	almonds, toasted

Preheat the oven to 180°C/350°F/Gas Mark 4. Oil a 20.5 cm/8 inch square tin and line with non-stick baking paper.

Sprinkle the sugar and the flaked almonds over the paper, then arrange the apricot halves cut-side down on top.

Cream the butter and sugar together in a large bowl until light and fluffy. Gradually beat the eggs into the butter mixture, adding a spoonful of flour after each addition of egg.

When all the eggs have been added, stir in the remaining flour and ground almonds and mix thoroughly. Add the almond essence and the apricots and stir well.

Spoon the mixture into the prepared tin, taking care not to dislodge the apricot halves. Bake in the preheated oven for 1 hour, or until golden and firm to touch.

Remove from the oven and allow to cool slightly for 15–20 minutes. Turn out carefully, discard the lining paper and transfer to a serving dish. Pour the honey over the top of the cake, sprinkle on the toasted almonds and serve.

Try this: FOR AN ALTERNATIVE: 164   FOR KIDS: 168

Buttery Passion Fruit Madeira Cake

CUTS INTO 8-10 SLICES

210 g/7½ oz plain flour
1 tsp baking powder
175 g/6 oz unsalted
   butter, softened

250 g/9 oz caster sugar
grated zest of 1 orange
1 tsp vanilla essence
3 medium eggs, beaten

2 tbsp milk
6 ripe passion fruits
50 g/2 oz icing sugar
icing sugar, to dust

Preheat the oven to 180°C/350°F/Gas Mark 4, 10 minutes before baking. Lightly oil and line the base of a 23 x 12.5 cm/9 x 5 inch loaf tin with greaseproof paper. Sift the flour and baking powder into a bowl and reserve.

Beat the butter, sugar, orange zest and vanilla essence until light and fluffy, then gradually beat in the eggs, 1 tablespoon at a time, beating well after each addition. If the mixture appears to curdle or separate, beat in a little of the flour mixture.

Fold in the flour mixture with the milk until just blended. Do not over mix. Spoon lightly into the prepared tin and smooth the top evenly. Sprinkle lightly with an extra teaspoon of caster sugar.

Bake in the preheated oven for 55 minutes, or until well risen and golden brown. Remove from the oven and leave to cool for 15–20 minutes. Turn the cake out of the tin and discard the lining paper.

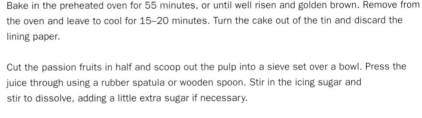

Cut the passion fruits in half and scoop out the pulp into a sieve set over a bowl. Press the juice through using a rubber spatula or wooden spoon. Stir in the icing sugar and stir to dissolve, adding a little extra sugar if necessary.

Using a skewer, pierce holes all over the cake. Slowly spoon the passion fruit glaze over the cake and allow to seep in. Gently invert the cake on to a wire rack, then turn it back the right way up. Dust with icing sugar and cool completely. Serve the Madeira cake cold.

Try this: FOR AN ALTERNATIVE: 204 FOR KIDS: 186

Coffee & Walnut Gateau with Brandied Prunes

CUTS INTO 10-12 SLICES

For the prunes:
225 g/8 oz ready-to-eat
    pitted dried prunes
150 ml/¼ pint cold tea
3 tbsp brandy

For the cake:
450 g/1 lb walnut pieces

50 g/2 oz self-raising flour
½ tsp baking powder
1 tsp instant coffee powder
    (not granules)
5 large eggs, separated
¼ tsp cream of tartar
150 g/5 oz caster sugar
2 tbsp sunflower oil

8 walnut halves, to decorate

For the filling:
600 ml/1 pint double cream
4 tbsp icing sugar, sifted
2 tbsp coffee-flavoured
    liqueur

Preheat the oven to 180°C/350°F/Gas Mark 4, 10 minutes before baking. Put the prunes in a small bowl with the tea and brandy and allow to stand for 3–4 hours or overnight. Oil and line the bases of two 23 cm/9 inch cake tins. Chop the walnut pieces in a food processor and reserve a quarter of them. Add the flour, baking powder and coffee and blend until finely ground.

Whisk the egg whites with the cream of tartar until soft peaks form. Sprinkle in one-third of the sugar, 2 tablespoons at a time, until stiff peaks form. In another bowl, beat the egg yolks, oil and the remaining sugar, until thick. Using a metal spoon or rubber spatula, alternately fold in the nut mixture and egg whites until just blended. Divide the mixture evenly between the tins, smoothing the tops. Bake in the preheated oven for 30–35 minutes, or until the top of the cakes spring back when lightly pressed. When cool, remove from the tins.

Drain the prunes, reserving the soaking liquid. Dry on kitchen paper, then chop and reserve. Whisk the cream with the icing sugar and liqueur until soft peaks form. Spoon one-eighth of the cream into a pastry bag fitted with a star nozzle. Cut the cake layers in half horizontally. Sprinkle each cut side with 1 tablespoon of the prune-soaking liquid. Sandwich the cakes together with half the cream and all the chopped prunes. Spread the remaining cream around the sides of the cake and press in the reserved chopped walnuts. Pipe rosettes around the edge of the cake and serve.

Try this: FOR AN ALTERNATIVE: 62   FOR KIDS: 26

Almond Cake

CUTS INTO 8 SLICES

225 g/8 oz butter or
  margarine
225 g/8 oz caster sugar
3 large eggs

1 tsp vanilla essence
1 tsp almond essence
125 g/4 oz self-raising flour
175 g/6 oz ground almonds

50 g/2 oz whole
  almonds, blanched
25 g/1 oz plain dark
  chocolate

Preheat the oven to 150°C/300°F/Gas Mark 2. Lightly oil and line the base of a 20.5 cm/ 8 inch deep round cake tin with greaseproof or baking paper.

Cream together the butter or margarine and sugar with a wooden spoon until light and fluffy. Beat the eggs and essences together. Gradually add to the sugar and butter mixture and mix well between each addition.

Sift the flour and mix with the ground almonds. Beat into the egg mixture until mixed well and smooth. Pour into the prepared cake tin. Roughly chop the whole almonds and scatter over the cake.

Bake in the preheated oven for 45 minutes, or until golden and risen and a skewer inserted into the centre of the cake comes out clean. Remove from the tin and leave to cool on a wire rack.

Melt the chocolate in a small bowl placed over a saucepan of gently simmering water, stirring until smooth and free of lumps. Drizzle the melted chocolate over the cooled cake and serve once the chocolate has set.

Try this: FOR AN ALTERNATIVE: 44   FOR KIDS: 28

Banana Cake

CUTS INTO 8 SLICES

3 medium-sized ripe bananas
1 tsp lemon juice
150 g/5 oz soft brown sugar
75 g/3 oz butter
   or margarine

250 g/9 oz self-raising flour
1 tsp ground cinnamon
3 medium eggs
50 g/2 oz walnuts, chopped
1 tsp each ground cinnamon

and caster sugar,
   to decorate
fresh cream, to serve

Preheat the oven to 190°C/375°F/Gas Mark 5, 10 minutes before baking. Lightly oil and line the base of a deep 18 cm/7 inch round cake tin with greaseproof or baking paper.

Mash two of the bananas in a small bowl, sprinkle with the lemon juice and a heaped tablespoon of the sugar. Mix together lightly and reserve.

Gently heat the remaining sugar and butter or margarine in a small saucepan until the butter has just melted. Pour into a small bowl, then allow to cool slightly. Sift the flour and cinnamon into a large bowl and make a well in the centre.

Beat the eggs into the cooled sugar mixture, pour into the well of flour, and mix thoroughly. Gently stir in the mashed banana mixture. Pour half of the mixture into the prepared tin. Thinly slice the remaining banana and arrange over the cake mixture. Sprinkle over the chopped walnuts, then cover with the remaining cake mixture.

Bake in the preheated oven for 50–55 minutes, or until well risen and golden brown. Allow to cool in the tin, turn out and sprinkle with the ground cinnamon and caster sugar. Serve hot or cold with a jug of fresh cream for pouring.

Try this: FOR AN ALTERNATIVE: 50 FOR KIDS: 158

Coffee & Pecan Cake

CUTS INTO 8 SLICES

175 g/6 oz self-raising flour
125 g/4 oz butter or margarine
175 g/6 oz golden caster sugar
1 tbsp instant coffee
    powder or granules
2 large eggs

50 g/2 oz pecans,
    roughly chopped

For the icing:
1 tsp instant coffee powder
    or granules

1 tsp cocoa powder
75 g/3 oz unsalted
    butter, softened
175 g/6 oz icing sugar, sifted
whole pecans, to decorate

Preheat the oven to 190°C/375°F/Gas Mark 5, 10 minutes before baking. Lightly oil and line the bases of two 18 cm/7 inch sandwich tins with greaseproof paper. Sift the flour and reserve.

Beat the butter or margarine and sugar together until light and creamy. Dissolve the coffee in 2 tablespoons of hot water and allow to cool. Lightly mix the eggs with the coffee liquid. Gradually beat into the creamed butter and sugar, adding a little of the sifted flour with each addition.

Fold in the pecans, then divide the mixture between the prepared tins and bake in the preheated oven for 20–25 minutes, or until well risen and firm to the touch. Leave to cool in the tins for 5 minutes before turning out and cooling on a wire rack.

To make the icing, blend together the coffee and cocoa powder with enough boiling water to make a stiff paste. Beat into the butter and icing sugar.

Sandwich the two cakes together using half of the icing. Spread the remaining icing over the top of the cake and decorate with the whole pecans to serve. Store in an airtight tin.

Gingerbread

CUTS INTO 8 SLICES

175 g/6 oz butter or margarine
225 g/8 oz black treacle
50 g/2 oz dark
   muscovado sugar

350 g/12 oz plain flour
2 tsp ground ginger
150 ml/¼ pint milk, warmed
2 medium eggs

1 tsp bicarbonate of soda
1 piece of stem ginger
   in syrup
1 tbsp stem ginger syrup

Preheat the oven to 150°C/300°C/Gas Mark 2, 10 minutes before baking. Lightly oil and line the base of a deep 20.5 cm/8 inch round cake tin with greaseproof paper.

In a saucepan gently heat the butter or margarine, black treacle and sugar, stirring occasionally until the butter melts. Leave to cool slightly.

Sift the flour and ground ginger into a large bowl. Make a well in the centre, then pour in the treacle mixture. Reserve 1 tablespoon of the milk, then pour the rest into the treacle mixture. Stir together lightly until mixed. Beat the eggs together, then stir into the mixture.

Dissolve the bicarbonate of soda in the remaining 1 tablespoon of warmed milk and add to the mixture. Beat the mixture until well mixed and free of lumps.

Pour into the prepared tin and bake in the preheated oven for 1 hour, or until well risen and a skewer inserted into the centre comes out clean.

Cool in the tin, then remove. Slice the stem ginger into thin slivers and sprinkle over the cake. Drizzle with the syrup and serve.

Celebration Fruit Cake

CUTS INTO 16 SLICES

125 g/4 oz butter or margarine
125 g/4 oz soft dark brown sugar
380 g can crushed pineapple
150 g/5 oz raisins
150 g/5 oz sultanas
125 g/4 oz crystallised
   ginger, finely chopped
125 g/4 oz glacé cherries,

coarsely chopped
125 g/4 oz mixed cut peel
225 g/8 oz self-raising flour
1 tsp bicarbonate of soda
2 tsp mixed spice
1 tsp ground cinnamon
½ tsp salt
2 large eggs, beaten

For the topping:
100 g/3½ oz pecan or walnut
   halves, lightly toasted
125 g/4 oz red, green and
   yellow glacé cherries
100 g/3½ oz small pitted
   prunes or dates
2 tbsp clear honey

Preheat the oven to 170°C/325°F/Gas Mark 3, 10 minutes before baking. Heat the butter and sugar in a saucepan until the sugar has dissolved, stirring frequently. Add the pineapple and juice, dried fruits and peel. Bring to the boil and simmer for 3 minutes, stirring occasionally. Remove from the heat to cool completely.

Lightly oil and line the base of a 20.5 x 7.5 cm/8 x 3 inch loose-bottomed cake tin with non-stick baking paper. Sift the flour, bicarbonate of soda, spices and salt into a bowl. Add the boiled fruit mixture to the flour with the eggs and mix. Spoon into the tin and smooth the top.

Bake in the preheated oven for 1¼ hours, or until a skewer inserted into the centre comes out clean. If the cake is browning too quickly, cover loosely with tinfoil and reduce the oven temperature. Remove and cool completely before removing from the tin and discarding the lining paper.

Arrange the nuts, cherries and prunes or dates in an attractive pattern on top of the cake. Heat the honey and brush over the topping to glaze. Alternatively, toss the nuts and fruits in the warm honey and spread evenly over the top of the cake. Cool completely and store in a cake tin for a day or two before serving to allow the flavours to develop.

Try this: FOR AN ALTERNATIVE: 68   FOR KIDS: 162

Orange Fruit Cake

CUTS INTO 10-12 SLICES

For the cake:
225 g/8 oz self-raising flour
2 tsp baking powder
225 g/8 oz caster sugar
225 g/8 oz butter, softened
4 large eggs
grated zest of 1 orange
2 tbsp orange juice
2–3 tbsp Cointreau

125 g/4 oz chopped nuts
Cape gooseberries,
    blueberries, raspberries
    and mint sprigs to
    decorate
icing sugar, to dust (optional)

For the filling:
450 ml/¾ pint double cream

50 ml/2 fl oz Greek yogurt
½ tsp vanilla essence
2–3 tbsp Cointreau
1 tbsp icing sugar
450 g/1 lb orange fruits, such
    as mango, peach,
    nectarine, papaya and
    yellow plums

Preheat the oven to 180°C/350°F/Gas Mark 4, 10 minutes before baking. Line the base of a 25.5 cm/10 inch ring mould tin or deep springform tin with non-stick baking paper. Sift the flour and baking powder into a large bowl and stir in the sugar. Make a well in the centre and add the butter, eggs, grated zest and orange juice. Beat until blended and a smooth batter is formed. Turn into the tin and smooth the top.

Bake in the preheated oven for 35–45 minutes, or until golden and the sides begin to shrink from the edge of the tin. Cool before removing from the tin. Using a serrated knife, cut the cake horizontally about one third from the top and remove the top layer of the cake. If not using a ring mould tin, scoop out a centre ring of sponge from the top third and the bottom two thirds of the layer, making a hollow tunnel. Sprinkle the cut sides with the Cointreau.

For the filling, whip the cream and yogurt with the vanilla essence, Cointreau and icing sugar until soft peaks form. Chop the orange fruit and fold into the cream. Spoon some of this mixture on to the bottom cake layer. Transfer to a serving plate. Cover with the top layer of sponge and spread the remaining cream mixture over the top and sides. Press the chopped nuts into the sides of the cake and decorate the top with fruit. Dust the top with icing sugar.

Try this: FOR AN ALTERNATIVE: 44   FOR KIDS: 70

Whisked Sponge Cake

CUTS INTO 6 SLICES

125 g/4 oz plain flour, plus 1 tsp	3 medium eggs	50 g/2 oz fresh
175 g/6 oz caster sugar,	1 tsp vanilla essence	raspberries, crushed
plus 1 tsp	4 tbsp raspberry jam	icing sugar, to dust

Preheat the oven to 200°C/400°F/Gas Mark 6, 15 minutes before baking. Mix 1 teaspoon of the flour and 1 teaspoon of the sugar together. Lightly oil two 18 cm/7 inch sandwich tins and dust lightly with the sugar and flour.

Place the eggs in a large heatproof bowl. Add the sugar, then place over a saucepan of gently simmering water ensuring that the base of the bowl does not touch the hot water. Using an electric whisk beat the sugar and eggs until they become light and fluffy. The whisk should leave a trail in the mixture when it is lifted out.

Remove the bowl from the saucepan of water, add the vanilla essence and continue beating for 2–3 minutes. Sift the flour gently into the egg mixture and using a metal spoon or rubber spatula carefully fold in, taking care not to over mix and remove all the air that has been whisked in.

Divide the mixture between the two prepared cake tins. Tap lightly on the work surface to remove any air bubbles. Bake in the preheated oven for 20–25 minutes, or until golden. Test that the cake is ready by gently pressing the centre with a clean finger – it should spring back.

Leave to cool in the tins for 5 minutes, then turn out on to a wire rack. Blend the jam and the crushed raspberries together. When the cakes are cold spread over the jam mixture and sandwich together. Dust the top with icing sugar and serve.

Try this: FOR AN ALTERNATIVE: 86 FOR KIDS: 24

Lemon Drizzle Cake

CUTS INTO 16 SQUARES

125 g/4 oz butter or margarine	2 large eggs	unwaxed
175 g/6 oz caster sugar	175 g/6 oz self-raising flour	50 g/2 oz granulated sugar
	2 lemons, preferably	

Preheat the oven to 180°C/350°F/Gas Mark 4, 10 minutes before baking. Lightly oil and line the base of an 18 cm/7 inch square cake tin with baking paper.

In a large bowl, cream the butter or margarine and sugar together until soft and fluffy. Beat the eggs, then gradually add a little of the egg to the creamed mixture, adding 1 tablespoon of flour after each addition.

Finely grate the rind from 1 of the lemons and stir into the creamed mixture, beating well until smooth. Squeeze the juice from the lemon, strain, then stir into the mixture.

Spoon into the prepared tin, level the surface and bake in the preheated oven for 25–30 minutes. Using a zester, remove the peel from the last lemon and mix with 25 g/1 oz of the granulated sugar and reserve.

Squeeze the juice into a small saucepan. Add the rest of the granulated sugar to the lemon juice in the saucepan and heat gently, stirring occasionally. When the sugar has dissolved, simmer gently for 3–4 minutes until syrupy.

With a cocktail stick or fine skewer prick the cake all over. Sprinkle the lemon zest and sugar over the top of the cake, drizzle over the syrup and leave to cool in the tin. Cut the cake into squares and serve.

Try this: FOR AN ALTERNATIVE: 36 FOR KIDS: 38

Toffee Walnut Swiss Roll

CUTS INTO 10-12 SLICES

4 large eggs, separated
½ tsp cream of tartar
125 g/4 oz icing sugar, plus
extra to dust
½ tsp vanilla essence
125 g/4 oz self-raising flour

For the toffee
walnut filling:
2 tbsp plain flour
150 ml/¼ pint milk
5 tbsp golden syrup or
maple syrup

2 large egg yolks, beaten
100 g/3½ oz walnuts
or pecans, toasted
and chopped
300 ml/½ pint double
cream, whipped

Preheat the oven to 190°C/375°F/Gas Mark 5, 10 minutes before baking. Lightly oil and line a Swiss roll tin with non-stick baking paper. Beat the egg whites and cream of tartar until softly peaking. Gradually beat in 50 g/2 oz of the icing sugar until stiff peaks form. In another bowl, beat the egg yolks with the remaining icing sugar until thick. Beat in the vanilla essence. Gently fold in the flour and egg whites alternately using a metal spoon or rubber spatula.

Spoon the batter into the tin and spread evenly. Bake in the preheated oven for 12 minutes, or until well risen and golden and the cake springs back when pressed with a clean finger. Lay a clean tea towel on a work surface and lay a piece of baking paper about 33 cm/13 inches long on the towel and dust with icing sugar. As soon as the cake is cooked turn out on to the paper. Peel off the lining paper and cut off the crisp edges of the cake. Starting at one narrow end, roll the cake with the paper and towel. Transfer to a wire rack and cool completely.

For the filling, put the flour, milk and syrup into a small saucepan and place over a gentle heat. Bring to the boil, whisking until thick and smooth. Remove from the heat and slowly beat into the beaten egg yolks. Pour the mixture back into the saucepan and cook over a low heat until it thickens and coats the back of a spoon. Strain the mixture into a bowl and stir in the chopped walnuts or pecans. Cool, stirring occasionally, then fold in about half of the whipped cream. Unroll the cooled cake and spread the filling over the cake. Re-roll and decorate with the remaining cream. Sprinkle with the icing sugar and serve.

Try this: FOR AN ALTERNATIVE: 84   FOR KIDS: 106

Almond Angel Cake with Amaretto Cream

CUTS INTO 10-12 SLICES

175 g/6 oz icing sugar, plus
    2–3 tbsp
150 g/5 oz plain flour
350 ml/12 fl oz egg whites
    (about 10 large egg whites)

1½ tsp cream of tartar
½ tsp vanilla essence
1 tsp almond essence
¼ tsp salt
200 g/7 oz caster sugar

175 ml/6 fl oz double cream
2 tablespoons
    Amaretto liqueur
fresh raspberries,
    to decorate

Preheat the oven to 180°C/350°F/Gas Mark 4, 10 minutes before baking. Sift together the 175 g/6 oz icing sugar and flour. Stir to blend, then sift again and reserve. Using an electric whisk, beat the egg whites, cream of tartar, vanilla essence, ½ teaspoon of almond essence and salt on medium speed until soft peaks form. Gradually add the caster sugar, 2 tablespoons at a time, beating well after each addition, until stiff peaks form.

Sift about one third of the flour mixture over the egg white mixture and using a metal spoon or rubber spatula, gently fold into the egg white mixture. Repeat, folding the flour mixture into the egg white mixture in two more batches. Spoon gently into an ungreased angel food cake tin or 25.5 cm/10 inch tube tin.

Bake in the preheated oven until risen and golden on top and the surface springs back quickly when gently pressed with a clean finger. Immediately invert the cake tin and cool completely in the tin. When cool, carefully run a sharp knife around the edge of the tin and the centre ring to loosen the cake from the edge. Ease the cake from the tin and invert on to a cake plate. Thickly dust the cake with the extra icing sugar.

Whip the cream with the remaining almond essence, Amaretto liqueur and a little more icing sugar, until soft peaks form. Fill a piping bag fitted with a star nozzle with half the cream and pipe around the bottom edge of the cake. Decorate the edge with the fresh raspberries and serve the remaining cream separately.

Try this: FOR AN ALTERNATIVE: 58 FOR KIDS: 30

Wild Strawberry & Rose Petal Jam Cake

CUTS INTO 8 SERVINGS

275 g/10 oz plain flour
1 tsp baking powder
¼ tsp salt
150 g/5 oz unsalted
 butter, softened
200 g/7 oz caster sugar
2 large eggs, beaten
2 tbsp rosewater

125 ml/4 fl oz milk
125 g/4 oz rose petal or
 strawberry jam,
 slightly warmed
125 g/4 oz wild strawberries,
 hulled, or baby
 strawberries, chopped
frosted rose petals, to decorate

For the rose cream filling:
200 ml/7 fl oz double cream
25 ml/1 fl oz natural
 Greek yogurt
2 tbsp rosewater
1–2 tbsp icing sugar

Preheat the oven to 180°C/350°F/Gas Mark 4, 10 minutes before baking. Lightly oil and flour a 20.5 cm/8 inch non-stick cake tin.

Sift the flour, baking powder and salt into a bowl and reserve. In another bowl, beat the butter and sugar until light and fluffy. Beat in the eggs, a little at a time, then stir in the rosewater. Gently fold in the flour mixture and milk with a metal spoon or rubber spatula and mix lightly together. Spoon the cake mixture into the tin, spreading evenly and smoothing the top.

Bake in the preheated oven for 25–30 minutes, or until well risen and golden and the centre springs back when pressed with a clean finger. Remove and cool, then remove from the tin.

For the filling, whisk the cream, yogurt, 1 tablespoon of rosewater and 1 tablespoon of icing sugar until soft peaks form. Split the cake horizontally in half and sprinkle with the remaining rosewater. Spread the warmed jam on the base of the cake. Top with half the whipped cream mixture, then sprinkle with half the strawberries. Place the remaining cake half on top. Spread with the remaining cream and swirl, if desired. Decorate with the rose petals. Dust the cake lightly with a little icing sugar and serve.

Raspberry & Hazelnut Meringue Cake

CUTS INTO 8 SERVINGS

For the meringue:
4 large egg whites
¼ tsp cream of tartar
225 g/8 oz caster sugar
75 g/3 oz hazelnuts, skinned,
    toasted and finely ground

For the filling:
300 ml/½ pint double cream
1 tbsp icing sugar
1–2 tbsp raspberry-flavoured
    liqueur (optional)
350 g/12 oz fresh raspberries

Preheat the oven to 140°C/275°F/Gas Mark 1. Line two baking sheets with non-stick baking paper and draw a 20.5 cm/8 inch circle on each.

Whisk the egg whites and cream of tartar until soft peaks form then gradually beat in the sugar, 2 tablespoons at a time. Beat well after each addition until the whites are stiff and glossy. Using a metal spoon or rubber spatula, gently fold in the ground hazelnuts.

Divide the mixture evenly between the two circles and spread neatly. Swirl one of the circles to make a decorative top layer. Bake in the preheated oven for about 1½ hours, until crisp and dry. Turn off the oven and allow the meringues to cool for 1 hour. Transfer to a wire rack to cool completely. Carefully peel off the papers.

For the filling, whip the cream, icing sugar and liqueur, if using, together until soft peaks form. Place the flat round on a serving plate. Spread over most of the cream, reserving some for decorating, and arrange the raspberries in concentric circles over the cream.

Place the swirly meringue on top of the cream and raspberries, pressing down gently. Pipe the remaining cream on to the meringue, decorate with a few raspberries and serve.

Try this: FOR AN ALTERNATIVE: 272   FOR KIDS: 228

Fruity Roulade

SERVES 4

For the sponge:
3 medium eggs
75 g/3 oz caster sugar
75 g/3 oz plain flour, sieved
1–2 tbsp caster sugar
   for sprinkling

For the filling:
125 g/4 oz Quark
125 g/4 oz half-fat
   Greek yogurt
25 g/1 oz caster sugar
1 tbsp orange

liqueur (optional)
grated rind of 1 orange
125 g/4 oz strawberries,
   hulled and cut
   into quarters, plus extra
   to decorate

Preheat the oven to 220°C/425°F/Gas Mark 7. Lightly oil and line a 33 x 23 cm/13 x 9 inch Swiss roll tin with greaseproof paper.

Using an electric whisk, whisk the eggs and sugar until the mixture is doubled in volume and leaves a trail across the top. Fold in the flour with a metal spoon or rubber spatula. Pour into the prepared tin and bake in the preheated oven for 10–12 minutes, until well risen and golden.

Place a whole sheet of greaseproof paper on a flat work surface and sprinkle evenly with caster sugar.

Turn the cooked sponge out on to the paper, discard the paper, trim the sponge and roll up encasing the paper inside. Reserve until cool.

To make the filling, mix together the Quark, yogurt, caster sugar, liqueur (if using) and orange rind. Unroll the roulade and spread over the mixture. Scatter over the strawberries and roll up. Decorate the roulade with the strawberries. Dust with the icing sugar and serve.

Try this: FOR AN ALTERNATIVE: 74 FOR KIDS: 220

Swiss Roll

CUTS INTO 8 SLICES

75 g/3 oz self-raising flour
3 large eggs
1 tsp vanilla essence
90 g/3½ oz caster sugar

25 g/1 oz hazelnuts, toasted
    and finely chopped
3 tbsp apricot conserve
300 ml/½ pint double cream,

lightly whipped
50 g/2 oz icing sugar
1–1½ tbsp lemon juice

Preheat the oven to 220°C/425°F/Gas Mark 7, 15 minutes before baking. Lightly oil and line the base of a 23 x 33 cm/9 x 13 inch Swiss roll tin with a single sheet of greaseproof or baking paper. Sift the flour several times, then reserve on top of the oven to warm a little.

Place a mixing bowl with the eggs, vanilla essence and sugar over a saucepan of hot water, ensuring that the base of the bowl is not touching the water. With the saucepan off the heat, whisk with an electric hand whisk until the egg mixture becomes pale and mousse-like and has increased in volume.

Remove the basin from the saucepan and continue to whisk for a further 2–3 minutes. Sift in the flour and very gently fold in using a metal spoon or rubber spatula, being careful not to knock out the air whisked in already. Pour into the prepared tin, tilting to ensure that the mixture is evenly distributed. Bake in the preheated oven for 10–12 minutes, or until well risen, golden brown and the top springs back when touched lightly with a clean finger.

Sprinkle the toasted, chopped hazelnuts over a large sheet of greaseproof paper. When the cake has cooked, turn out on to the hazelnut covered paper and trim the edges of the cake. Holding an edge of the paper with the short side of the cake nearest you, roll the cake up.

When fully cold, carefully unroll and spread with the jam and then the cream. Roll back up and serve. Otherwise, store in the refrigerator and eat within two days.

Try this: FOR AN ALTERNATIVE: 96 FOR KIDS: 40

Fresh Strawberry Sponge Cake

8-10 SERVINGS

175 g/6 oz unsalted
  butter, softened
175 g/6 oz caster sugar
1 tsp vanilla essence

3 large eggs, beaten
175 g/6 oz self-raising flour
150 ml/¼ pint double cream
2 tbsp icing sugar, sifted

225 g/8 oz fresh strawberries,
  hulled and chopped
few extra strawberries,
  to decorate

Preheat the oven to 190°C/375°F/Gas Mark 5, 10 minutes before baking. Lightly oil and line the bases of two 20.5 cm/8 inch round cake tins with greaseproof paper.

Using an electric whisk, beat the butter, sugar and vanilla essence until pale and fluffy. Gradually beat in the eggs a little at a time, beating well between each addition. Sift half the flour over the mixture and, using a metal spoon or rubber spatula, gently fold into the mixture. Sift over the remaining flour and fold in until just blended.

Divide the mixture between the tins, spreading evenly. Gently smooth the surfaces with the back of a spoon. Bake in the centre of the preheated oven for 20–25 minutes, or until well risen and golden.

Remove and leave to cool before turning out on to a wire rack. Whip the cream with 1 tablespoon of the icing sugar until it forms soft peaks. Fold in the chopped strawberries.

Spread one cake layer evenly with the mixture and top with the second cake layer, rounded side up. Thickly dust the cake with icing sugar and decorate with the reserved strawberries. Carefully slide on to a serving plate and serve.

Try this: FOR AN ALTERNATIVE: 76 FOR KIDS: 24

Crunchy Rhubarb Crumble

SERVES 6

125 g/4 oz plain flour	50 g/2 oz demerara sugar	450 g/1 lb fresh rhubarb
50 g/2 oz softened butter	1 tbsp sesame seeds	50 g/2 oz caster sugar
50 g/2 oz rolled oats	½ tsp ground cinnamon	custard or cream, to serve

Preheat the oven to 180°C/350°F/Gas Mark 4. Place the flour in a large bowl and cut the butter into cubes. Add to the flour and rub in with your fingertips until the mixture looks like fine breadcrumbs, or blend for a few seconds in a food processor. Stir in the rolled oats, demerara sugar, sesame seeds and cinnamon. Mix well and reserve.

Prepare the rhubarb by removing the thick ends of the stalks and cut diagonally into 2.5 cm/ 1 inch chunks. Wash thoroughly and pat dry with a clean tea towel. Place the rhubarb in a 1.1 litre/2 pint pie dish.

Sprinkle the caster sugar over the rhubarb and top with the reserved crumble mixture. Level the top of the crumble so that all the fruit is well covered and press down firmly. If liked, sprinkle the top with a little extra caster sugar.

Place on a baking sheet and bake in the preheated oven for 40–50 minutes, or until the fruit is soft and the topping is golden brown. Sprinkle the pudding with some more caster sugar and serve hot with custard or cream.

Try this: FOR AN ALTERNATIVE: 250   FOR KIDS: 96

Osborne Pudding

SERVES 4

8 slices of white bread
50 g/2 oz butter
2 tbsp marmalade
50 g/2 oz luxury mixed
    dried fruit
2 tbsp fresh orange juice

40 g/1½ oz caster sugar
2 large eggs
450 ml/¾ pint milk
150 ml/¼ pint
    whipping cream

For the marmalade sauce:
zest and juice of 1 orange
2 tbsp thick-cut
    orange marmalade
1 tbsp brandy (optional)
2 tsp cornflour

Preheat the oven to 170°C/325°F/Gas Mark 3. Lightly oil a 1.1 litre/2 pint baking dish.

Remove the crusts from the bread and spread thickly with butter and marmalade. Cut the bread into small triangles. Place half the bread in the base of the dish and sprinkle over the dried mixed fruit, 1 tablespoon of the orange juice and half the caster sugar.

Top with the remaining bread and marmalade, buttered side up and pour over the remaining orange juice. Sprinkle over the remaining caster sugar. Whisk the eggs with the milk and cream and pour over the pudding. Reserve for about 30 minutes to allow the bread to absorb the liquid.

Place in a roasting tin and pour in enough boiling water to come halfway up the sides of the dish. Bake in the preheated oven for 50–60 minutes, or until the pudding is set and the top is crisp and golden.

Meanwhile, make the marmalade sauce. Heat the orange zest and juice with the marmalade and brandy if using. Mix 1 tablespoon of water with the cornflour and mix together well. Add to the saucepan and cook on a low heat, stirring until warmed through and thickened. Serve the pudding hot with the marmalade sauce.

Try this: FOR AN ALTERNATIVE: 110   FOR KIDS: 114

Queen of Puddings

SERVES 4

75 g/3 oz fresh white breadcrumbs	450 ml/¾ pint full-cream milk	2 medium eggs, separated
25 g/1 oz granulated sugar	25 g/1 oz butter	2 tbsp seedless raspberry jam
	grated rind of 1 small lemon	50 g/2 oz caster sugar

Preheat the oven to 170°C/325°F/Gas Mark 3. Oil a 900 ml/1½ pint ovenproof baking dish and reserve.

Mix the breadcrumbs and sugar together in a bowl. Pour the milk into a small saucepan and heat gently with the butter and lemon rind until the butter has melted. Allow the mixture to cool a little, then pour over the breadcrumbs. Stir well and leave to soak for 30 minutes.

Whisk the egg yolks into the cooled breadcrumb mixture and pour into the prepared dish. Place the dish on a baking sheet and bake in the preheated oven for about 30 minutes, or until firm and set. Remove from the oven.

Allow to cool slightly, then spread the jam over the pudding. Whisk the egg whites until stiff and standing in peaks.

Gently fold in the caster sugar with a metal spoon or rubber spatula. Pile the meringue over the top of the pudding.

Return the dish to the oven for a further 25–30 minutes, or until the meringue is crisp and just slightly coloured. Serve hot or cold.

Try this: FOR AN ALTERNATIVE: 120   FOR KIDS: 228

Lemon Surprise

SERVES 4

75 g/3 oz margarine
175 g/6 oz caster sugar
3 medium eggs, separated
75 g/3 oz self-raising flour

450 ml/¾ pint semi-
   skimmed milk
juice of 2 lemons
juice of 1 orange

2 tsp icing sugar
lemon twists, to decorate
sliced strawberries,
   to serve

Preheat the oven to 190°C/375°F/Gas Mark 5. Lightly oil a deep ovenproof dish.

Beat together the margarine and sugar until pale and fluffy. Add the egg yolks, one at a time, with 1 tablespoon of the flour and beat well after each addition. Once added, stir in the remaining flour. Stir in the milk, 4 tablespoons of the lemon juice and 3 tablespoons of the orange juice.

Whisk the egg whites until stiff and fold into the pudding mixture with a metal spoon or rubber spatula until well combined. Pour into the prepared dish.

Stand the dish in a roasting tin and pour in just enough boiling water to come halfway up the sides of the dish. Bake in the preheated oven for 45 minutes, until well risen and spongy to the touch.

Remove the pudding from the oven and sprinkle with the icing sugar. Decorate with the lemon twists and serve immediately with the strawberries.

Try this: FOR AN ALTERNATIVE: 100   FOR KIDS: 108

Oaty Fruit Puddings

SERVES 4

125 g/4 oz rolled oats
50 g/2 oz butter, melted
2 tbsp chopped almonds
1 tbsp clear honey
pinch of ground cinnamon

2 pears, peeled,
   cored and
   finely chopped
1 tbsp marmalade
orange zest, to decorate

custard or fruit-flavoured
   yogurt, to serve

Preheat the oven to 200°C/400°F/Gas Mark 6. Lightly oil and line the bases of four individual pudding bowls or muffin tins with a small circle of greaseproof paper.

Mix together the oats, butter, nuts, honey and cinnamon in a small bowl. Using a spoon, spread two thirds of the oaty mixture over the base and around the sides of the pudding bowls or muffin tins.

Toss together the pears and marmalade and spoon into the oaty cases. Scatter over the remaining oaty mixture to cover the pears and marmalade.

Bake in the preheated oven for 15–20 minutes, until cooked and the tops of the puddings are golden and crisp.

Leave for 5 minutes before removing the pudding bowls or the muffin tins. Decorate with orange zest and serve hot with custard or fruit-flavoured yogurt.

Try this: FOR AN ALTERNATIVE: 88   FOR KIDS: 112

Eve's Pudding

SERVES 6

450 g/1 lb cooking apples
175 g/6 oz blackberries
75 g/3 oz demerara sugar
grated rind of 1 lemon

125 g/4 oz caster sugar
125 g/4 oz butter
few drops of vanilla essence
2 medium eggs, beaten

125 g/4 oz self-raising flour
1 tbsp icing sugar
ready-made custard,
to serve

Preheat the oven to 180°C/350°F/Gas Mark 4. Oil a 1.1 litre/2 pint baking dish.

Peel, core and slice the apples and place a layer in the base of the prepared dish. Sprinkle over some of the blackberries, a little demerara sugar and lemon zest. Continue to layer the apple and blackberries in this way until all the ingredients have been used.

Cream the sugar and butter together until light and fluffy. Beat in the vanilla essence and then the eggs a little at a time, adding a spoonful of flour after each addition. Fold in the extra flour with a metal spoon or rubber spatula and mix well. Spread the sponge mixture over the top of the fruit and level with the back of a spoon.

Place the dish on a baking sheet and bake in the preheated oven for 35–40 minutes, or until well risen and golden brown. To test if the pudding is cooked, press the cooked sponge lightly with a clean finger – if it springs back the sponge is cooked.

Dust the pudding with a little icing sugar and serve immediately with the custard.

Try this: FOR AN ALTERNATIVE: 90   FOR KIDS: 42

Lemon & Apricot Pudding

SERVES 4

125 g/4 oz ready-to-eat
   dried apricots
3 tbsp orange juice, warmed
50 g/2 oz butter

125 g/4 oz caster sugar
juice and grated rind of
   2 lemons
2 medium eggs

50 g/2 oz self-raising flour
300 ml/½ pint milk
custard or fresh cream,
   to serve

Preheat the oven to 180°C/350°F/Gas Mark 4. Oil a 1.1 litre/2 pint pie dish.

Soak the apricots in the orange juice for 10–15 minutes or until most of the juice has been absorbed, then place in the base of the pie dish.

Cream the butter and sugar together with the lemon rind until light and fluffy. Separate the eggs. Beat the egg yolks into the creamed mixture with a spoonful of flour after each addition. Add the remaining flour and beat well until smooth.

Stir the milk and lemon juice into the creamed mixture. Whisk the egg whites in a grease-free mixing bowl until stiff and standing in peaks. Fold into the mixture using a metal spoon or rubber spatula.

Pour into the prepared dish and place in a baking tray filled with enough cold water to come halfway up the sides of the dish.

Bake in the preheated oven for about 45 minutes, or until the sponge is firm and golden brown. Remove from the oven. Serve immediately with the custard or fresh cream.

Try this: FOR AN ALTERNATIVE: 94 FOR KIDS: 214

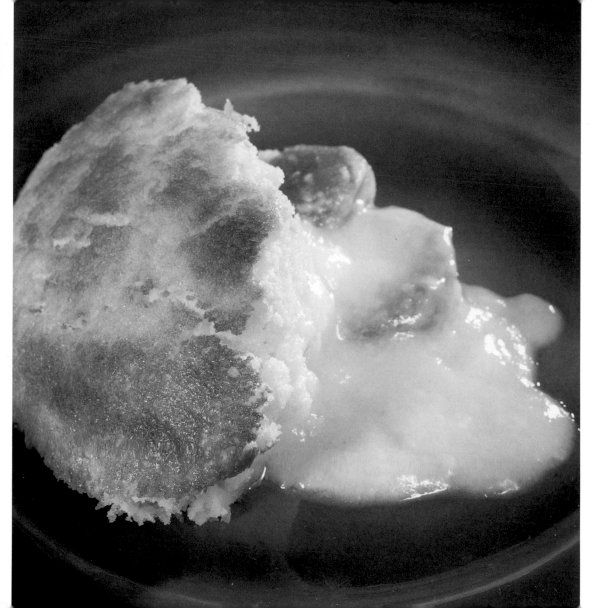

Rich Double–crust Plum Pie

SERVES 6

For the pastry:
75 g/3 oz butter
75 g/3 oz white vegetable fat
225 g/8 oz plain flour

2 medium egg yolks

For the filling:
450 g/1 lb fresh plums,

preferably Victoria
50 g/2 oz caster sugar
1 tbsp milk
a little extra caster sugar

Preheat the oven to 200°C/400°F/Gas Mark 6. Make the pastry by rubbing the butter and white vegetable fat into the flour until it resembles fine breadcrumbs, or blend in a food processor. Add the egg yolks and enough water to make a soft dough. Knead lightly, then wrap and leave in the refrigerator for about 30 minutes.

Meanwhile, prepare the fruit. Rinse and dry the plums, then cut in half and remove the stones. Slice the plums into chunks and cook in a saucepan with 25 g/1 oz of the sugar and 2 tablespoons of water for 5–7 minutes, or until slightly softened. Remove from the heat, add the remaining sugar to taste and allow to cool.

Roll out half the chilled pastry on a lightly floured surface and use to line the base and sides of a 1.1 litre/2 pint pie dish. Allow the pastry to hang over the edge of the dish. Spoon in the prepared plums. Roll out the remaining pastry to use as the lid and brush the edge with a little water. Wrap the pastry around the rolling pin and place over the plums.

Press the edges together to seal and mark a decorative edge around the rim of the pastry by pinching with your thumb and forefinger or using the back of a fork.

Brush the lid with milk, and make a few slits in the top. Use any trimmings to decorate the top of the pie with pastry leaves. Place on a baking sheet and bake in the preheated oven for 30 minutes, or until golden brown. Sprinkle with a little caster sugar and serve hot or cold.

Try this: FOR AN ALTERNATIVE: 234 FOR KIDS: 208

Baked Apple Dumplings

SERVES 4

225 g/8 oz self-raising flour
¼ tsp salt
125 g/4 oz shredded suet

4 medium cooking apples
4–6 tsp luxury mincemeat
1 medium egg white, beaten

2 tsp caster sugar
custard or vanilla sauce,
   to serve

Preheat the oven to 200°C/400°F/Gas Mark 6. Lightly oil a baking tray.

Place the flour and salt in a bowl and stir in the suet. Add just enough water to the mixture to mix to a soft but not sticky dough, using the fingertips. Turn the dough on to a lightly floured board and knead lightly into a ball.

Divide the dough into four pieces and roll out each piece into a thin square, large enough to encase the apples.

Peel and core the apples and place one apple in the centre of each square of pastry. Fill the centre of the apple with mincemeat, brush the edges of each pastry square with water and draw the corners up to meet over each apple.

Press the edges of the pastry firmly together and decorate with pastry leaves and shapes made from the extra pastry trimmings.

Place the apples on the prepared baking tray, brush with the egg white and sprinkle with the sugar. Bake in the preheated oven for 30 minutes or until golden and the pastry and apples are cooked. Serve the dumplings hot with the custard or vanilla sauce.

Try this: FOR AN ALTERNATIVE: 96   FOR KIDS: 34

Jam Roly Poly

SERVES 6

225 g/8 oz self-raising flour
¼ tsp salt
125 g/4 oz shredded suet

about 150 ml/¼ pint water
3 tbsp strawberry jam
1 tbsp milk, to glaze

1 tsp caster sugar
ready-made jam sauce,
    to serve

Preheat the oven to 200°C/400°F/Gas Mark 6.

Make the pastry by sifting the flour and salt into a large bowl. Add the suet and mix lightly, then add the water a little at a time and mix to form a soft and pliable dough – take care not to make the dough too wet.

Turn the dough out on to a lightly floured board and knead gently until smooth. Roll the dough out into a 23 x 28 cm/9 x 11 inch rectangle. Spread the jam over the pastry leaving a border of 1 cm/½ inch all round. Fold the border over the jam and brush the edges with water.

Lightly roll the rectangle up from one of the short sides, seal the top edge and press the ends together. Do not roll the pudding up too tightly. Turn the pudding upside down on to a large piece of greaseproof paper large enough to come halfway up the sides.

Tie the ends of the paper, to make a boat-shaped paper case for the pudding to sit in and to leave plenty of room for the roly poly to expand.

Brush the pudding lightly with milk and sprinkle with the sugar. Bake in the preheated oven for 30–40 minutes, or until well risen and golden. Serve immediately with the jam sauce.

Try this: FOR AN ALTERNATIVE: 220   FOR KIDS: 118

Golden Castle Pudding

SERVES 4-6

125 g/4 oz butter	vanilla essence	4 tbsp golden syrup
125 g/4 oz caster sugar	2 medium eggs, beaten	crème fraîche or ready-made
a few drops of	125 g/4 oz self-raising flour	custard, to serve

Preheat the oven to 180°C/350°F/Gas Mark 4. Lightly oil four to six individual pudding bowls and place a small circle of lightly oiled non-stick greaseproof paper in the base of each one.

Place the butter and caster sugar in a large bowl, then beat together until the mixture is pale and creamy. Stir in the vanilla essence and gradually add the beaten eggs, a little at a time. Add a tablespoon of flour after each addition of egg and beat well.

When the mixture is smooth, add the remaining flour and fold in gently. Add a tablespoon of water and mix to form a soft mixture that will drop easily off a spoon.

Spoon enough mixture into each basin to come halfway up the tin, allowing enough space for the puddings to rise. Place on a baking sheet and bake in the preheated oven for about 25 minutes until firm and golden brown.

Allow the puddings to stand for 5 minutes. Discard the paper circles and turn out on to individual serving plates.

Warm the golden syrup in a small saucepan and pour a little over each pudding. Serve hot with the crème fraîche or custard.

Try this: FOR AN ALTERNATIVE: 210   FOR KIDS: 116

College Pudding

SERVES 4

125 g/4 oz shredded suet
125 g/4 oz fresh
  white breadcrumbs
50 g/2 oz sultanas

50 g/2 oz seedless raisins
½ tsp ground cinnamon
¼ tsp freshly grated nutmeg
¼ tsp mixed spice

50 g/2 oz caster sugar
½ tsp baking powder
2 medium eggs, beaten
orange zest, to garnish

Preheat the oven to 180°C/350°F/Gas Mark 4. Lightly oil an ovenproof 900 ml/1½ pint ovenproof pudding basin and place a small circle of greaseproof paper in the base.

Mix the shredded suet and breadcrumbs together and rub lightly together with the fingertips to remove any lumps.

Stir in the dried fruit, spices, sugar and baking powder. Add the eggs and beat lightly together until the mixture is well blended and the fruit is evenly distributed.

Spoon the mixture into the prepared pudding basin and level the surface. Place on a baking tray and cover lightly with some greaseproof paper.

Bake in the preheated oven for 20 minutes, then remove the paper and continue to bake for a further 10–15 minutes, or until the top is firm.

When the pudding is cooked, remove from the oven and carefully turn out on to a warmed serving dish. Decorate with the orange zest and serve immediately.

Try this: FOR AN ALTERNATIVE: 234 FOR KIDS: 226

Apple & Cinnamon Brown Betty

SERVES 4

450 g/1 lb cooking apples
50 g/2 oz caster sugar
finely grated rind of 1 lemon
125 g/4 oz fresh white
    breadcrumbs

125 g/4 oz demerara sugar
½ tsp ground cinnamon
25 g/1 oz butter
For the custard:
3 medium egg yolks

1 tbsp caster sugar
500 ml/1 pint milk
1 tbsp cornflour
few drops of vanilla essence

Preheat the oven to 180°C/350°F/Gas Mark 4. Lightly oil a 900 ml/1½ pint ovenproof dish.

Peel, core and slice the apples and place in a saucepan with the caster sugar, lemon rind and 2 tablespoons of water. Simmer for 10–15 minutes or until tender.

Mix the breadcrumbs with the sugar and the cinnamon. Place half the sweetened apples in the base of the prepared dish and spoon over half of the crumb mixture. Place the remaining apples on top and cover with the rest of the crumb mixture.

Melt the butter and pour over the surface of the pudding. Cover the dish with non-stick baking paper and bake in the preheated oven for 20 minutes. Remove the paper and bake for a further 10–15 minutes, or until golden.

Meanwhile, make the custard by whisking the egg yolks and sugar together until creamy. Mix 1 tablespoon of the milk with the cornflour until a paste forms and reserve.

Warm the rest of the milk until nearly boiling and pour over the egg mixture with the paste and vanilla essence. Place the bowl over a saucepan of gently simmering water. Stir over the heat until thickened and able to coat the back of a spoon. Strain into a jug and serve hot over the pudding.

Try this: FOR AN ALTERNATIVE: 104   FOR KIDS: 46

Lattice Treacle Tart

SERVES 4

For the pastry:
175 g/6 oz plain flour
40 g/1½ oz butter
40 g/1½ oz white vegetable fat

For the filling:
225 g/8 oz golden syrup
finely grated rind and juice
of 1 lemon

75 g/3 oz fresh white
breadcrumbs
1 small egg, beaten

Preheat the oven to 190°C/375°F/Gas Mark 5.

Make the pastry by placing the flour, butter and white vegetable fat in a food processor. Blend in short, sharp bursts until the mixture resembles fine breadcrumbs. Remove from the processor and place on a pastry board or in a large bowl. Stir in enough cold water to make a dough and knead in a large bowl or on a floured surface until smooth and pliable.

Roll out the pastry and use to line a 20.5 cm/8 inch loose-bottomed fluted flan tin. Reserve the pastry trimmings for decoration and chill for 30 minutes.

Meanwhile, to make the filling, place the golden syrup in a saucepan and warm gently with the lemon rind and juice. Tip the breadcrumbs into the pastry case and pour the syrup mixture over the top.

Roll the pastry trimmings out on a lightly floured surface and cut into 6–8 thin strips. Lightly dampen the pastry edge of the tart, then place the strips across the filling in a lattice pattern. Brush the ends of the strips with water and seal to the edge of the tart. Brush a little beaten egg over the pastry and bake in the preheated oven for a 25 minutes, or until the filling is just set. Serve hot or cold.

Try this: FOR AN ALTERNATIVE: 236 FOR KIDS: 240

Iced Bakewell Tart

CUTS INTO 8 SLICES

For the rich pastry:
175 g/6 oz plain flour
pinch of salt
60 g/2½ oz butter, cut into
    small pieces
50 g/2 oz white vegetable fat,
    cut into small pieces

2 small egg yolks, beaten

For the filling:
125 g/4 oz butter, melted
125 g/4 oz caster sugar
125 g/4 oz ground almonds
2 large eggs, beaten

few drops of almond essence
2 tbsp seedless raspberry jam

For the icing:
125 g/4 oz icing sugar, sifted
6–8 tsp fresh lemon juice
25 g/1 oz toasted flaked almonds

Preheat the oven to 200°C/400°F/Gas Mark 6.

Place the flour and salt in a bowl and rub in the butter and vegetable fat until the mixture resembles breadcrumbs. Alternatively, blend quickly in short bursts in a food processor. Add the eggs with sufficient water to make a soft, pliable dough. Knead lightly on a floured board then chill in the refrigerator for about 30 minutes. Roll out the pastry and use to line a 23 cm/9 inch loose-bottomed flan tin.

For the filling, mix together the melted butter, sugar, almonds and beaten eggs and add a few drops of almond essence. Spread the base of the pastry case with the raspberry jam and spoon over the egg mixture.

Bake in the preheated oven for about 30 minutes, or until the filling is firm and golden brown. Remove from the oven and allow to cool completely.

When the tart is cold make the icing by mixing together the icing sugar and lemon juice, a little at a time, until the icing is smooth and of a spreadable consistency. Spread the icing over the tart, leave to set for 2–3 minutes and sprinkle with the almonds. Chill in the refrigerator for about 10 minutes and serve.

Try this: FOR AN ALTERNATIVE: 242   FOR KIDS: 298

Mocha Pie

SERVES 4-6

1 x 23 cm/9 inch ready-made
   sweet pastry case

For the filling:
125 g/4 oz plain dark
   chocolate, broken
   into pieces

175g/6 oz unsalted butter
225 g/8 oz soft brown sugar
1 tsp vanilla essence
3 tbsp strong black coffee

For the topping:
600 ml/1 pint double cream

50 g/2 oz icing sugar
2 tsp vanilla essence
1 tsp instant coffee
   dissolved in 1 tsp boiling
   water and cooled
grated plain and white
   chocolate, to decorate

Place the prepared pastry case on a large serving plate and reserve. Melt the chocolate in a heatproof bowl set over a saucepan of simmering water. Ensure the water is not touching the base of the bowl. Remove from the heat, stir until smooth and leave to cool.

Cream the butter, soft brown sugar and vanilla essence until light and fluffy, then beat in the cooled chocolate. Add the strong black coffee, pour into the pastry case and chill in the refrigerator for about 30 minutes.

For the topping, whisk the cream until beginning to thicken, then whisk in the sugar and vanilla essence. Continue to whisk until the cream is softly peaking. Spoon just under half of the cream into a separate bowl and fold in the dissolved coffee.

Spread the remaining cream over the filling in the pastry case. Spoon the coffee-flavoured whipped cream evenly over the top, then swirl it decoratively with a palate knife. Sprinkle with grated chocolate and chill in the refrigerator until ready to serve.

Try this: FOR AN ALTERNATIVE: 294 FOR KIDS: 270

Topsy Turvy Pudding

SERVES 6

For the topping:
175 g/6 oz demerara sugar
2 oranges

For the sponge:
175 g/6 oz butter, softened

175 g/6 oz caster sugar
3 medium eggs, beaten
175 g/6 oz self-raising
   flour, sifted
50 g/2 oz plain dark
   chocolate, melted

grated rind of 1 orange
25 g/1 oz cocoa
   powder, sifted
custard or soured cream,
   to serve

Preheat the oven to 180°C/350°F/Gas Mark 4, 10 minutes before baking. Lightly oil a 20.5 cm/8 inch deep round loose-based cake tin. Place the demerara sugar and 3 tablespoons of water in a small, heavy-based saucepan and heat gently until the sugar has dissolved. Swirl the saucepan or stir with a clean wooden spoon to ensure the sugar has dissolved, then bring to the boil and boil rapidly until a golden caramel is formed. Pour into the base of the tin and leave to cool.

For the sponge, cream the butter and sugar together until light and fluffy. Gradually beat in the eggs a little at a time, beating well between each addition. Add a spoonful of flour after each addition to prevent the mixture curdling. Add the melted chocolate and then stir well. Fold in the orange rind, self-raising flour and sifted cocoa powder and mix well.

Remove the peel from both oranges taking care to remove as much of the pith as possible. Thinly slice the peel into strips and then slice the oranges. Arrange the peel and then the orange slices over the caramel. Top with the sponge mixture and level the top.

Place the tin on a baking sheet and bake in the preheated oven for 40–45 minutes or until well risen, golden brown and an inserted skewer comes out clean. Remove from the oven, leave for about 5 minutes, invert onto a serving plate and sprinkle with cocoa powder. Serve with either custard or soured cream.

Try this: FOR AN ALTERNATIVE: 254 FOR KIDS: 310

Fudgy Mocha Pie with Espresso Custard Sauce

CUTS INTO 10 SLICES

125 g/4 oz plain dark
  chocolate, chopped
125 g/4 oz butter, diced
1 tbsp instant espresso
  powder
4 large eggs
1 tbsp golden syrup
125 g/4 oz sugar

1 tsp ground cinnamon
3 tbsp milk
icing sugar, for dusting
few fresh strawberries,
  to serve

For th custard sauce:
2–3 tbsp instant espresso

powder, or to taste
225 ml/8 fl oz prepared
  custard sauce
225 ml/8 fl oz single cream
2 tbsp coffee-flavoured
  liqueur (optional)

Preheat the oven to 180°C/350°F/Gas Mark 4, 10 minutes before serving. Lightly oil a deep 23 cm/9 inch pie plate or line with tinfoil.

Melt the chocolate and butter in a small saucepan over a low heat and stir until smooth, then reserve. Dissolve the instant espresso powder in 1–2 tablespoons of hot water and reserve.

Beat the eggs with the golden syrup, the sugar, the dissolved espresso powder, the cinnamon and milk until blended. Add the melted chocolate mixture and whisk until blended. Pour into the pie plate.

Bake the pie in the preheated oven for about 20–25 minutes, or until the edge has set but the centre is still very soft. Leave to cool, remove from plate then dust lightly with icing sugar.

To make the custard sauce, dissolve the instant espresso powder with 2–3 tablespoons of hot water, then whisk into the prepared custard sauce. Slowly add the single cream, whisking constantly, then stir in the coffee-flavoured liqueur, if using. Serve slices of the pie in a pool of espresso custard with strawberries.

Try this: FOR AN ALTERNATIVE: 120 FOR KIDS: 294

Egg Custard Tart

SERVES 6

For the sweet pastry:
50 g/2 oz butter
50 g/2 oz white vegetable fat
175 g/6 oz plain flour

1 medium egg yolk, beaten
2 tsp caster sugar
For the filling:
300 ml/½ pint milk

2 medium eggs, plus
1 medium egg yolk
25 g/1 oz caster sugar
½ tsp freshly grated nutmeg

Preheat the oven to 200°C/400°F/Gas Mark 6. Oil a 20.5 cm/8 inch flan tin or dish.

Make the pastry by cutting the butter and vegetable fat into small cubes. Add to the flour in a large bowl and rub in, until the mixture resembles fine breadcrumbs. Add the egg, sugar and enough water to form a soft and pliable dough. Turn on to a lightly floured board and knead. Wrap and chill in the refrigerator for 30 minutes.

Roll the pastry out on to a lightly floured surface or pastry board and use to line the oiled flan tin. Place in the refrigerator to reserve.

Warm the milk in a small saucepan. Briskly whisk together the eggs, egg yolk and caster sugar. Pour the milk into the egg mixture and whisk until blended. Strain through a sieve into the pastry case.

Place the flan tin on a baking sheet. Sprinkle the top of the tart with nutmeg and bake in the preheated oven for about 15 minutes.

Turn the oven down to 170°C/325°F/Gas Mark 3 and bake for a further 30 minutes, or until the custard has set. Serve hot or cold.

Try this: FOR AN ALTERNATIVE: 282   FOR KIDS: 296

Strawberry Flan

SERVES 6

For the sweet pastry:
175 g/6 oz plain flour
50 g/2 oz butter
50 g/2 oz white vegetable fat
2 tsp caster sugar
1 medium egg yolk, beaten

For the filling:
1 medium egg, plus 1 extra
    egg yolk
50 g/2 oz caster sugar
25 g/1 oz plain flour
300 ml/½ pint milk

few drops of vanilla essence
450 g/1 lb strawberries,
    cleaned and hulled
mint leaves, to decorate

Preheat the oven to 200°C/400°F/Gas Mark 6. Place the flour, butter and vegetable fat in a food processor and blend until the mixture resembles fine breadcrumbs. Stir in the sugar, then with the machine running, add the egg yolk and enough water to make a fairly stiff dough. Knead lightly, cover and chill in the refrigerator for 30 minutes.

Roll out the pastry and use to line a 23 cm/9 inch loose -bottomed flan tin. Place a piece of greaseproof paper in the pastry case and cover with baking beans or rice. Bake in the preheated oven for 15–20 minutes, until just firm. Reserve until cool.

Make the filling by whisking the eggs and sugar together until thick and pale. Gradually stir in the flour and then the milk. Pour into a small saucepan and simmer for 3–4 minutes, stirring throughout.

Add the vanilla essence to taste, then pour into a bowl and leave to cool. Cover with greaseproof paper to prevent a skin from forming.

When the filling is cold, whisk until smooth then pour on to the cooked flan case. Slice the strawberries and arrange on the top of the filling. Decorate with the mint leaves and serve.

Crème Brûlée with Sugared Raspberries

SERVES 6

600 ml/1 pint fresh
    whipping cream
4 medium egg yolks

75 g/3 oz caster sugar
½ tsp vanilla essence
25 g/1 oz demerara sugar

175 g/6 oz fresh raspberries

Preheat the oven to 150°C/300°F/Gas Mark 2. Pour the cream into a bowl and place over a saucepan of gently simmering water. Heat gently but do not allow to boil.

Meanwhile, whisk together the egg yolks, 50 g/2 oz of the caster sugar and the vanilla essence. When the cream is warm, pour it over the egg mixture briskly whisking until it is mixed completely.

Pour into six individual ramekin dishes and place in a roasting tin. Fill the tin with sufficient water to come halfway up the sides of the dishes.

Bake in the preheated oven for about 1 hour, or until the puddings are set. To test if set, carefully insert a round bladed knife into the centre. If the knife comes out clean they are set.

Remove the puddings from the roasting tin and allow to cool. Chill in the refrigerator, preferably overnight.

Sprinkle the sugar over the top of each dish and place the puddings under a preheated hot grill. When the sugar has caramelised and turned deep brown, remove from the heat and cool. Chill the puddings in the refrigerator for 2–3 hours before serving.

Toss the raspberries in the remaining caster sugar and sprinkle over the top of each dish. Serve with a little extra cream if liked.

Try this: FOR AN ALTERNATIVE: 306   FOR KIDS: 264

Baked Lemon & Sultana Cheesecake

CUTS INTO 10 SLICES

275 g/10 oz caster sugar
50 g/2 oz butter
50 g/2 oz self-raising flour
½ level tsp baking powder
5 large eggs
450 g/1 lb cream cheese

40 g/1½ oz plain flour
grated rind of 1 lemon
3 tbsp fresh lemon juice
150 ml/¼ pint crème fraîche
75 g/3 oz sultanas

To decorate:
1 tbsp icing sugar
fresh blackcurrants or
    blueberries
mint leaves

Preheat the oven to 170°C/325°F/Gas Mark 3. Oil a 20.5 cm/8 inch loose-bottomed round cake tin with non-stick baking paper.

Beat 50 g/2 oz of the sugar and the butter together until light and creamy, then stir in the self-raising flour, baking powder and 1 egg. Mix lightly together until well blended. Spoon into the prepared tin and spread the mixture over the base. Separate the four remaining eggs and reserve.

Blend the cheese in a food processor until soft. Gradually add the eggs yolks and sugar and blend until smooth. Turn into a bowl and stir in the rest of the flour, lemon rind and juice. Mix lightly before adding the crème fraîche and sultanas, stirring well.

Whisk the egg whites until stiff, fold into the cheese mixture and pour into the tin. Tap lightly on the surface to remove any air bubbles. Bake in the preheated oven for about 1 hour, or until golden and firm. Cover lightly if browning too much. Switch the oven off and leave in the oven to cool for 2–3 hours.

Remove the cheesecake from the oven and, when completely cold, remove from the tin. Sprinkle with the icing sugar, decorate with the blackcurrants or blueberries and mint leaves and serve.

Try this: FOR AN ALTERNATIVE: 262   FOR KIDS: 254

Chocolate

Honey & Chocolate Hearts

MAKES ABOUT 20

60 g/2½ oz caster sugar
15 g/½ oz butter
125 g/4 oz thick honey
1 small egg, beaten

pinch of salt
1 tbsp mixed peel or
   chopped glacé ginger
¼ tsp ground cinnamon

pinch of ground cloves
225 g/8 oz plain flour, sifted
½ tsp baking powder, sifted
75 g/3 oz milk chocolate

Preheat the oven to 220°C/425°F/Gas Mark 7, 15 minutes before baking. Lightly oil two baking sheets. Heat the sugar, butter and honey together in a small saucepan until everything has melted and the mixture is smooth.

Remove from the heat and stir until slightly cooled, then add the beaten egg with the salt and beat well. Stir in the mixed peel or glacé ginger, ground cinnamon, ground cloves, the flour and the baking powder and mix well until a dough is formed. Wrap in clingfilm and chill in the refrigerator for 45 minutes.

Place the chilled dough on a lightly floured surface, roll out to about 5 mm/¼ inch thickness and cut out small heart shapes. Place onto the prepared baking sheets and bake in the preheated oven for 8–10 minutes. Remove from the oven and leave to cool slightly. Using a spatula, transfer to a wire rack until cold.

Melt the chocolate in a heatproof bowl set over a saucepan of simmering water. Alternatively, melt the chocolate in the microwave according to the manufacturer's instructions, until smooth. Dip one half of each biscuit in the melted chocolate. Leave to set before serving.

Chocolate Shortcake

MAKES 30-32

225 g/8 oz unsalted
   butter, softened
150 g/5 oz icing sugar

1 tsp vanilla essence
250 g/9 oz plain flour
25 g/1 oz cocoa powder

¼ tsp salt
extra icing sugar,
   to decorate

Preheat the oven to 170°C/325°F/Gas Mark 3, 10 minutes before baking. Lightly oil several baking sheets and line with non-stick baking parchment. Place the butter, icing sugar and vanilla essence together in a food processor and blend briefly until smooth. Alternatively, using a wooden spoon, cream the butter, icing sugar and vanilla essence in a large bowl.

Sift the flour, cocoa powder and salt together then either add to the food processor bowl and blend quickly to form a dough, or add to the bowl and, using your hands, mix together until a smooth dough is formed.

Turn the dough out onto a clean board lined with clingfilm. Place another sheet of clingfilm over the top and roll the dough out until it is 1 cm/½ inch thick. Transfer the whole board to the refrigerator and chill for 1½–2 hours.

Remove the top piece of clingfilm and use a 5 cm/2 inch cutter to cut the dough into 30–32 rounds. Place the rounds on the prepared baking sheets and bake in the preheated oven for about 15 minutes or until firm.

Cool for 1 minute, then using a spatula, carefully remove the shortcakes from the baking parchment and transfer to a wire rack. Leave to cool completely. Sprinkle the shortcakes with sifted icing sugar before serving. Store in an airtight tin for a few days.

Chocolate Macaroons

MAKES 20

650 g/2½ oz plain
   dark chocolate
125 g/4 oz ground almonds

125 g/4 oz caster sugar
¼ tsp almond essence
1 tbsp cocoa powder

2 medium egg whites
1 tbsp icing sugar

Preheat the oven to 180°C/350°F/Gas Mark 4, 10 minutes before baking. Lightly oil several baking sheets and line with sheets of non-stick baking parchment. Melt the chocolate in a heatproof bowl set over a saucepan of simmering water. Alternatively, melt in the microwave according to the manufacturer's instructions. Stir until smooth, then cool slightly.

Place the ground almonds in a food processor and add the sugar, almond essence, cocoa powder and 1 of the egg whites. Add the melted chocolate and a little of the other egg white and blend to make a soft, smooth paste. Alternatively, place the ground almonds with the sugar, almond essence and cocoa powder in a bowl and make a well in the centre. Add the melted chocolate with sufficient egg white and gradually blend together to form a smooth but not sticky paste.

Shape the dough into small balls the size of large walnuts and place them on the prepared baking sheets. Flatten them slightly, then brush with a little water. Sprinkle over a little icing sugar and bake in the preheated oven for 10–12 minutes or until just firm.

Using a spatula, carefully lift the macaroons off the baking parchment and transfer to a wire rack to cool. These are best served immediately, but can be stored in an airtight container.

Try this: FOR AN ALTERNATIVE: 30 FOR KIDS: 28

Chocolate & Ginger Florentines

MAKES 14-16

40 g/1½ oz butter
5 tbsp double cream
50 g/2 oz caster sugar
60 g/2½ oz chopped almonds

25 g/1 oz flaked almonds
40 g/1½ oz glacé
   ginger, chopped
25 g/1 oz plain flour

pinch of salt
150 g/5 oz plain
   dark chocolate

Preheat the oven to 180°C/350°F/Gas Mark 4, 10 minutes before baking. Lightly oil several baking sheets.

Melt the butter, cream and sugar together in a saucepan and bring slowly to the boil. Remove from the heat and stir in the almonds and the glacé ginger.

Leave to cool slightly, then mix in the flour and the salt. Blend together, then place heaped teaspoons of the mixture on the baking sheets. Make sure they are spaced well apart as they expand during cooking. Flatten them slightly with the back of a wet spoon.

Bake in the preheated oven for 10–12 minutes or until just brown at the edges. Leave to cool slightly. Using a spatula, carefully transfer to a wire rack and leave to cool.

Melt the chocolate in a heatproof bowl set over a saucepan of gently simmering water. Alternatively, melt the chocolate in the microwave according to the manufacturer's instructions, until just liquid and smooth. Spread thickly over one side of the Florentines, then mark wavy lines through the chocolate using a fork and leave until firm.

Try this: FOR AN ALTERNATIVE: 156   FOR KIDS: 152

Chocolate–covered Flapjack

MAKES 24

215 g/7½ oz plain flour
150 g/5 oz rolled oats
225 g/8 oz light
   muscovado sugar

1 tsp bicarbonate of soda
pinch of salt
150 g/5 oz butter
2 tbsp golden syrup

250 g/9 oz plain
   dark chocolate
5 tbsp double cream

Preheat the oven to 180°C/350°F/Gas Mark 4, 10 minutes before baking. Lightly oil a 33 x 23 cm/13 x 9 inch Swiss roll tin and line with non-stick baking parchment. Place the flour, rolled oats, the light muscovado sugar, bicarbonate of soda and salt into a bowl and stir well together.

Melt the butter and golden syrup together in a heavy-based saucepan and stir until smooth, then add to the oat mixture and mix together thoroughly. Spoon the mixture into the prepared tin, press down firmly and level the top.

Bake in the preheated oven for 15–20 minutes or until golden. Remove from the oven and leave the flapjack to cool in the tin. Once cool, remove from the tin. Discard the parchment.

Melt the chocolate in a heatproof bowl set over a saucepan of gently simmering water. Alternatively, melt the chocolate in the microwave according to the manufacturer's instructions. Once the chocolate has melted, quickly beat in the cream, then pour over the flapjack. Mark patterns over the chocolate with a fork when almost set.

Chill the flapjack in the refrigerator for at least 30 minutes before cutting into bars. When the chocolate has set, serve. Store in an airtight container for a few days.

Try this: FOR AN ALTERNATIVE: 32   FOR KIDS: 162

Chocolate Orange Biscuits

MAKES 30

100 g/3½ oz plain
    dark chocolate
125 g/4 oz butter
125 g/4 oz caster sugar

pinch of salt
1 medium egg, beaten
grated zest of 2 oranges
200 g/7 oz plain flour

1 tsp baking powder
125 g/4 oz icing sugar
1–2 tbsp orange juice

Preheat the oven to 200°C/400°F/Gas Mark 6, 15 minutes before baking. Lightly oil several baking sheets. Coarsely grate the chocolate and reserve. Beat the butter and sugar together until creamy. Add the salt, beaten egg and half the orange zest and beat again.

Sift the flour and baking powder, add to the bowl with the grated chocolate and beat to form a dough. Shape into a ball, wrap in clingfilm and chill in the refrigerator for 2 hours.

Roll the dough out on a lightly floured surface to 5 mm/¼ inch thickness and cut into 5 cm/ 2 inch rounds. Place the rounds on the prepared baking sheets, allowing room for expansion. Bake in the preheated oven for 10–12 minutes or until firm. Remove the biscuits from the oven and leave to cool slightly. Using a spatula, transfer to a wire rack and leave to cool.

Sift the icing sugar into a small bowl and stir in sufficient orange juice to make a smooth, spreadable icing. Spread the icing over the biscuits, leave until almost set, then sprinkle on the remaining grated orange zest before serving.

Try this: FOR AN ALTERNATIVE: 204   FOR KIDS: 154

Rum & Chocolate Squares

MAKES 14-16

125 g/4 oz butter	2 medium egg yolks	¼ tsp baking powder
100 g/3½ oz caster sugar	225 g/8 oz plain flour	2 tbsp cocoa powder
pinch of salt	50 g/2 oz cornflour	1 tbsp rum

Preheat the oven to 190°C/350°F/Gas Mark 5, 10 minutes before baking. Lightly oil several baking sheets. Cream the butter, sugar and salt together in a large bowl until light and fluffy. Add the egg yolks and beat well until smooth.

Sift together 175 g/6 oz of the flour, the cornflour and the baking powder, add to the mixture and mix well with a wooden spoon until a smooth and soft dough is formed.

Halve the dough and knead the cocoa powder into one half and the rum and the remaining plain flour into the other half. Place the two mixtures in two separate bowls, cover with clingfilm and chill in the refrigerator for 1 hour.

Roll out both pieces of dough separately on a well floured surface into two thin rectangles about 5 mm/¼ inch thick. Place one on top of the other, cut out squares approximately 5 cm/2 inch square and place on the prepared baking sheets.

Bake in the preheated oven, half with the chocolate uppermost and the other half, rum side up, for 10–12 minutes or until firm. Remove from the oven and leave to cool slightly. Using a spatula, transfer to a wire rack and leave to cool, then serve.

Try this: FOR AN ALTERNATIVE: 38   FOR KIDS: 138

Chocolate & Nut
Refrigerator Biscuits

MAKES 18

165 g/5½ oz slightly
   salted butter
150 g/5 oz soft dark
   brown sugar

25 g/1 oz granulated sugar
1 medium egg, beaten
200 g/7 oz plain flour
½ tsp bicarbonate of soda

25 g/1 oz cocoa powder
125 g/4 oz pecan nuts,
   finely chopped

Preheat the oven to 190°C/375°F/Gas Mark 5, 10 minutes before baking. Lightly grease several baking sheets with 15 g/½ oz of the butter. Cream the remaining butter and both sugars in a large bowl until light and fluffy, then gradually beat in the egg.

Sift the flour, bicarbonate of soda and cocoa powder together then gradually fold into the creamed mixture together with the chopped pecans. Mix thoroughly until a smooth but stiff dough is formed.

Place the dough on a lightly floured surface or pastry board and roll into sausage shapes about 5 cm/2 inches in diameter. Wrap in clingfilm and chill in the refrigerator for at least 12 hours, or preferably overnight.

Cut the dough into thin slices and place on the prepared baking sheets. Bake in the preheated oven for 8–10 minutes or until firm. Remove from the oven and leave to cool slightly. Using a spatula, transfer to a wire rack to cool. Store in an airtight tin.

Try this: FOR AN ALTERNATIVE: 138   FOR KIDS: 172

Chocolate Whirls

MAKES 20

125 g/4 oz soft margarine
75 g/3 oz unsalted
   butter, softened
75 g/3 oz icing sugar, sifted
75 g/3 oz plain dark

chocolate, melted
   and cooled
15 g/½ oz cornflour, sifted
125 g/4 oz plain flour
125 g/4 oz self-raising flour

For the buttercream:
125 g/4 oz unsalted
   butter, softened
½ tsp vanilla essence
225 g/8 oz icing sugar, sifted

Preheat the oven to 180°C/350°F/Gas Mark 4, 10 minutes before baking. Lightly oil two baking sheets.

Cream the margarine, butter and icing sugar together until the mixture is light and fluffy. Stir the chocolate until smooth, then beat into the creamed mixture. Stir in the cornflour. Sift the flours together, then gradually add to the creamed mixture, a little at a time, beating well between each addition. Beat until the consistency is smooth and stiff enough for piping.

Put the mixture in a piping bag fitted with a large star nozzle and pipe 40 small whirls onto the prepared baking sheets. Bake the whirls in the preheated oven for 12–15 minutes or until firm to the touch. Remove from the oven and leave to cool for about 2 minutes. Using a spatula, transfer the whirls to wire racks and leave to cool.

Meanwhile, make the buttercream. Cream the butter with the vanilla essence until soft. Gradually beat in the icing sugar and add a little cooled boiled water, if necessary, to give a smooth consistency. When the whirls are cold, pipe or spread on the prepared buttercream, sandwich together and serve.

Try this: FOR AN ALTERNATIVE: 140   FOR KIDS: 18

Chocolate Chip Cookies

MAKES ABOUT 30

140 g/4½ oz butter
50 g/2 oz caster sugar
60 g/2½ oz soft dark
   brown sugar

1 medium egg, beaten
½ tsp vanilla essence
125 g/4 oz plain flour
½ tsp bicarbonate of soda

150 g/5 oz plain or milk
   chocolate chips

Preheat the oven to 180°C/350°F/Gas Mark 4, 10 minutes before baking. Lightly butter 3–4 large baking sheets with 15 g/½ oz of the butter. Place the remaining butter and both sugars in a food processor and blend until smooth. Add the egg and vanilla essence and blend briefly. Alternatively, cream the butter and sugars together in a bowl, then beat in the egg with the vanilla essence.

If using a food processor, scrape out the mixture with a spatula and place the mixture into a large bowl. Sift the flour and bicarbonate of soda together, then fold into the creamed mixture. When the mixture is blended thoroughly, stir in the chocolate chips.

Drop heaped teaspoons of the mixture onto the prepared baking sheets, spaced well apart, and bake the cookies in the preheated oven for 10–12 minutes or until lightly golden.

Leave to cool for a few seconds, then using a spatula, transfer to a wire rack and cool completely. The cookies are best eaten when just cooked, but can be stored in an airtight tin for a few days.

Try this: FOR AN ALTERNATIVE: 162   FOR KIDS: 166

Chocolate Florentines

MAKES 20

125 g/4 oz butter or margarine
125 g/4 oz soft light
   brown sugar
1 tbsp double cream
50 g/2 oz blanched almonds,
   roughly chopped

50 g/2 oz hazelnuts,
   roughly chopped
75 g/3 oz sultanas
50 g/2 oz glacé cherries,
   roughly chopped
50 g/2 oz plain, dark

chocolate, roughly
   chopped or broken
50 g/2 oz milk chocolate,
   roughly chopped or broken
50 g/2 oz white chocolate,
   roughly chopped or broken

Preheat the oven to 180°C/350°F/Gas Mark 4, 10 minutes before baking. Lightly oil a baking sheet.

Melt the butter or margarine with the sugar and double cream in a small saucepan over a very low heat. Do not boil. Remove from the heat and stir in the almonds, hazelnuts, sultanas and cherries.

Drop teaspoonfuls of the mixture on to the baking sheet. Transfer to the preheated oven and bake for 10 minutes, until golden. Leave the biscuits to cool on the baking sheet for about 5 minutes, then carefully transfer to a wire rack to cool.

Melt the plain, milk and white chocolates in separate bowls, either in the microwave following the manufacturer's instructions or in a small bowl, placed over a saucepan of gently simmering water.

Spread one third of the biscuits with the plain chocolate, one third with the milk chocolate and one third with the white chocolate. Mark out wavy lines on the chocolate when almost set with the tines of a fork. Alternatively, dip some of the biscuits in chocolate to half coat and serve.

Try this: FOR AN ALTERNATIVE: 142   FOR KIDS: 174

Fudgy Chocolate Bars

MAKES 14

25 g/1 oz glacé cherries
60 g/2½ oz shelled hazelnuts
150 g/5 oz plain

dark chocolate
150 g/5 oz unsalted butter
¼ tsp salt

150 g/5 oz digestive biscuits
1 tbsp icing sugar,
sifted, optional

Preheat the oven to 180°C/350°F/Gas Mark 4, 10 minutes before baking. Lightly oil a 18 cm/7 inch square tin and line the base with non-stick baking parchment. Rinse the glacé cherries thoroughly, dry well on absorbent kitchen paper and reserve.

Place the nuts on a baking tray and roast in the preheated oven for 10 minutes, or until light golden brown. Leave to cool slightly, then chop roughly and reserve.

Break the chocolate into small pieces and place with the butter and salt in the top of a double boiler, or in a bowl set over a saucepan of gently simmering water. Heat gently, stirring, until melted and smooth. Alternatively, melt the chocolate in the microwave, according to the manufacturer's instructions.

Chop the biscuits into 5 mm/¼ inch pieces and cut the cherries in half. Add to the chocolate mixture with the nuts and stir well. Spoon the mixture into the prepared tin and level the top.

Chill in the refrigerator for 30 minutes, remove from the tin, discard the baking parchment and cut into 14 bars. Cover lightly, return to the refrigerator and keep chilled until ready to serve. To serve, lightly sprinkle the bars with sifted icing sugar, if using. Store the bars covered in the refrigerator.

Try this: FOR AN ALTERNATIVE: 170 FOR KIDS: 34

Fig & Chocolate Bars

MAKES 12

125 g/4 oz butter
150 g/5 oz plain flour
50 g/2 oz soft light

brown sugar
225 g/8 oz ready-to-eat
dried figs, halved

juice of ½ a large lemon
1 tsp ground cinnamon
125 g/4 oz plain dark chocolate

Preheat the oven to 180°C/350°F/Gas Mark 4, 10 minutes before baking. Lightly oil a 18 cm/7 inch square cake tin. Place the butter and the flour in a large bowl and, using your fingertips, rub the butter into the flour until it resembles fine breadcrumbs.

Stir in the sugar, then using your hands, bring the mixture together to form a smooth dough. Knead until smooth then press the dough into the prepared tin. Lightly prick the base with a fork and bake in the preheated oven for 20–30 minutes or until golden. Remove from the oven and leave the shortbread to cool in the tin until completely cold.

Meanwhile, place the dried figs, lemon juice, 125 ml/4 fl oz water and the ground cinnamon in a saucepan and bring to the boil. Cover and simmer for 20 minutes or until soft, stirring occasionally during cooking. Cool slightly, then purée in a food processor until smooth. Cool, then spread over the cooked shortbread.

Melt the chocolate in a heatproof bowl set over a saucepan of simmering water. Alternatively, the chocolate can be melted in the microwave, according to the manufacturer's instructions. Stir until smooth, then spread over the top of the fig filling. Leave to become firm, then cut into 12 bars and serve.

Try this: FOR AN ALTERNATIVE: 158 FOR KIDS: 178

Nanaimo Bars

MAKES 15

75 g/3 oz unsalted butter
125 g/4 oz plain
   dark chocolate,
   roughly chopped
75 g/3 oz digestive
   biscuits, crushed
75 g/3 oz desiccated coconut

50 g/2 oz chopped mixed nuts

For the filling:
1 medium egg yolk
1 tbsp milk
75 g/3 oz unsalted
   butter, softened

1 tsp vanilla essence
150 g/5 oz icing sugar

For the topping:
125 g/4 oz plain dark
   chocolate, chopped
2 tsp sunflower oil

Oil and line a 28 x 18 x 2.5 cm/11 x 7 x 1 inch cake tin with non-stick baking parchment. Place the butter and chocolate in a heatproof bowl set over a saucepan of almost boiling water until melted, stirring occasionally. Stir in the crushed biscuits, coconut and nuts into the chocolate mixture and mix well. Spoon into the prepared tin and press down firmly. Chill in the refrigerator for 20 minutes.

For the filling, place the egg yolk and milk in a heatproof bowl set over a saucepan of almost boiling water, making sure the bowl does not touch the water. Whisk for 2–3 minutes. Add the butter and vanilla essence to the bowl and continue whisking until fluffy, then gradually whisk in the icing sugar. Spread over the chilled base, smoothing with the back of a spoon and chill in the refrigerator for a further 30 minutes.

For the topping, place the chocolate and sunflower oil in a heatproof bowl set over a saucepan of almost boiling water. Melt, stirring occasionally, until smooth. Leave to cool slightly, then pour over the filling and tilt the tin, so that the chocolate spreads evenly.

Chill in the refrigerator for about 5 minutes, or until the chocolate topping is just set but not too hard, then mark into 15 bars. Chill again in the refrigerator for 2 hours, then cut into slices and serve.

Try this: FOR AN ALTERNATIVE: 170   FOR KIDS: 32

Chocolate Pecan Traybake

MAKES 12

175 g/6 oz butter
75 g/3 oz icing sugar, sifted
175 g/6 oz plain flour
25 g/1 oz self-raising flour
25 g/1 oz cocoa powder

For the pecan topping:
75 g/3 oz butter
50 g/2 oz light
   muscovado sugar
2 tbsp golden syrup

2 tbsp milk
1 tsp vanilla essence
2 medium eggs,
   lightly beaten
125 g/4 oz pecan halves

Preheat the oven to 180°C/350°F/Gas Mark 4, 10 minutes before baking. Lightly oil and line a 28 x 18 x 2.5 cm/11 x 7 x 1 inch cake tin with non-stick baking parchment.

Beat the butter and sugar together until light and fluffy. Sift in the flours and cocoa powder and mix together to form a soft dough.

Press the mixture evenly over the base of the prepared tin. Prick all over with a fork, then bake on the shelf above the centre of the preheated oven for 15 minutes.

Put the butter, sugar, golden syrup, milk and vanilla essence in a small saucepan and heat gently until melted. Remove from the heat and leave to cool for a few minutes, then stir in the eggs and pour over the base. Sprinkle with the nuts.

Bake in the preheated oven for 25 minutes or until dark golden brown, but still slightly soft. Leave to cool in the tin. When cool, carefully remove from the tin, then cut into 12 squares and serve. Store in an airtight container.

Try this: FOR AN ALTERNATIVE: 178 FOR KIDS: 158

Chocolate Biscuit Bars

SERVES 20

50 g/2 oz sultanas
3–4 tbsp brandy (optional)
100 g/3½ oz plain
   dark chocolate
125 g/4 oz unsalted butter
2 tbsp golden syrup

90 ml/3 fl oz double cream
6 digestive biscuits,
   roughly crushed
50 g/2 oz shelled pistachio
   nuts, toasted and
   roughly chopped

50 g/2 oz blanched almonds,
   toasted and chopped
50 g/2 oz glacé cherries,
   roughly chopped
grated zest of 1 orange
cocoa powder, sifted

Lightly oil a 20.5 cm/8 inch square tin and line with clingfilm.

Place the sultanas into a small bowl and pour over the brandy, if using. Leave to soak for 20–30 minutes.

Meanwhile, break the chocolate into small pieces and put into a heatproof bowl. Place the bowl over a saucepan of simmering water, making sure that the bottom of the bowl does not touch the water.

Leave the chocolate until melted, stirring occasionally. Remove from the heat. Add the butter, golden syrup and double cream to a small saucepan and heat until the butter has melted.

Remove the saucepan from the heat and add the melted chocolate, biscuits, nuts, cherries, orange zest, sultanas and the brandy mixture.

Mix thoroughly and pour into the prepared tin. Smooth the top and chill in the refrigerator for at least 4 hours, or until firm.

Turn out the cake and remove the clingfilm. Dust liberally with the cocoa powder then cut into bars to serve. Store lightly covered in the refrigerator.

Try this: FOR AN ALTERNATIVE: 36 FOR KIDS: 150

Light White Chocolate & Walnut Blondies

MAKES 15

75 g/3 oz unsalted butter
200 g/7 oz demerara sugar
2 large eggs, lightly beaten
1 tsp vanilla essence
2 tbsp milk

125 g/4 oz plain flour,
plus 1 tbsp
1 tsp baking powder
pinch of salt
75 g/3 oz walnuts,

roughly chopped
125 g/4 oz white
chocolate drops
1 tbsp icing sugar

Preheat the oven to 190°C/375°F/Gas Mark 5, 10 minutes before baking. Oil and line a 28 x 18 x 2.5 cm/11 x 7 x 1 inch cake tin with non-stick baking parchment.

Place the butter and demerara sugar into a heavy-based saucepan and heat gently until the butter has melted and the sugar has started to dissolve. Remove from the heat and leave to cool.

Place the eggs, vanilla essence and milk in a large bowl and beat together. Stir in the butter and sugar mixture, then sift in the 125 g/4oz of flour, the baking powder and salt. Gently stir the mixture twice.

Toss the walnuts and chocolate drops in the remaining 1 tablespoon of flour to coat. Add to the bowl and stir the ingredients together gently.

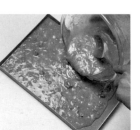

Spoon the mixture into the prepared tin and bake on the centre shelf of the preheated oven for 35 minutes, or until the top is firm and slightly crusty. Place the tin on a wire rack and leave to cool. When completely cold, remove the cake from the tin and lightly dust the top with icing sugar. Cut into 15 blondies, using a sharp knife, and serve.

Try this: FOR AN ALTERNATIVE: 172   FOR KIDS: 176

Miracle Bars

MAKES 12

100 g/3½ oz butter, melted, plus 1–2 tsp extra for oiling
125 g/4 oz digestive

biscuit crumbs
175 g/6 oz chocolate chips
75 g/3 oz shredded or desiccated coconut

125 g/4 oz chopped mixed nuts
400 g can sweetened condensed milk

Preheat the oven to 180°C/350°F/Gas Mark 4, 10 minutes before baking. Generously butter a 23 cm/9 inch square tin and line with non-stick baking paper.

Pour the butter into the prepared tin and sprinkle the biscuit crumbs over in an even layer. Add the chocolate chips, coconut and nuts in even layers and drizzle over the condensed milk.

Transfer the tin to the preheated oven and bake for 30 minutes, until golden brown. Allow to cool in the tin, then cut into 12 squares and serve.

Try this: FOR AN ALTERNATIVE: 168   FOR KIDS: 174

Chocolate Nut Brownies

MAKES 16

125 g/4 oz butter
150 g/5 oz soft light brown
   sugar, firmly packed
50 g/2 oz plain dark
   chocolate, roughly
   chopped or broken

2 tbsp smooth peanut butter
2 medium eggs
50 g/2 oz unsalted roasted
   peanuts, finely chopped
100 g/3 ½ oz self-raising
   flour

For the topping:
125 g/4 oz plain dark
   chocolate, roughly
   chopped or broken
50 ml/2 fl oz soured cream

Preheat the oven to 180°C/350°F/Gas Mark 4, 10 minutes before baking. Lightly oil and line a 20.5 cm/8 inch square cake tin with greaseproof paper.

Combine the butter, sugar and chocolate in a small saucepan and heat gently until the sugar and chocolate have melted, stirring constantly. Reserve and cool slightly.

Mix together the peanut butter, eggs and peanuts in a large bowl. Stir in the cooled chocolate mixture. Sift in the flour and fold together with a metal spoon or rubber spatula until combined.

Pour into the prepared tin and bake in the preheated oven for about 30 minutes, or until just firm. Cool for 5 minutes in the tin before turning out on to a wire rack to cool.

To make the topping, melt the chocolate in a heatproof bowl over a saucepan of simmering water, making sure that the base of the bowl does not touch the water.

Cool slightly, then stir in the soured cream until smooth and glossy. Spread over the brownies, refrigerate until set, then cut into squares. Serve the brownies cold.

Try this: FOR AN ALTERNATIVE: 168 FOR KIDS: 158

Marbled Chocolate Traybake

MAKES 18 SQUARES

175 g/6 oz butter
175 g/6 oz caster sugar
1 tsp vanilla essence
3 medium eggs,
    lightly beaten
200 g/7 oz self-raising flour

½ tsp baking powder
1 tbsp milk
1½ tbsp cocoa powder

For the chocolate icing:
75 g/3 oz plain dark

chocolate, broken
    into pieces
75 g/3 oz white chocolate,
    broken into pieces

Preheat the oven to 180°C/350°F/Gas Mark 4, 10 minutes before baking. Oil and line a 28 x 18 x 2.5 cm/11 x 7 x 1 inch cake tin with non-stick baking parchment.

Cream the butter, sugar and vanilla essence until light and fluffy. Gradually add the eggs, beating well after each addition. Sift in the flour and baking powder and fold in with the milk.

Spoon half the mixture into the prepared tin, spacing the spoonfuls apart and leaving gaps in between. Blend the cocoa powder to a smooth paste with 2 tablespoons of warm water. Stir this into the remaining cake mixture. Drop small spoonfuls between the vanilla cake mixture to fill in all the gaps. Use a knife to swirl the mixtures together a little.

Bake on the centre shelf of the preheated oven for 35 minutes, or until well risen and firm to the touch. Leave in the tin for 5 minutes to cool, then turn out onto a wire rack and leave to cool. Remove the parchment.

For the icing, place the plain and white chocolate in separate heatproof bowls and melt each over a saucepan of almost boiling water. Spoon into separate non-stick baking parchment piping bags, snip off the tips and drizzle over the top. Leave to set before cutting into squares.

Try this: FOR AN ALTERNATIVE: 192 FOR KIDS: 40

Triple Chocolate Brownies

MAKES 15

350 g/12 oz plain dark
  chocolate, broken
  into pieces
225 g/8 oz butter, cubed
225 g/8 oz caster sugar
3 large eggs, lightly beaten

1 tsp vanilla essence
2 tbsp very strong
  black coffee
100 g/3½ oz self-raising flour
125 g/4 oz pecans,
  roughly chopped

75 g/3 oz white chocolate,
  roughly chopped
75 g/3 oz milk chocolate,
  roughly chopped

Preheat the oven to 190°C/375°F/Gas Mark 5, 10 minutes before baking. Oil and line a 28 x 18 x 2.5 cm/11 x 7 x 1 inch cake tin with non-stick baking parchment.

Place the plain chocolate in a heatproof bowl with the butter set over a saucepan of almost boiling water, and stir occasionally until melted. Remove from the heat and leave until just cool, but not beginning to set.

Place the caster sugar, eggs, vanilla essence and coffee in a large bowl and beat together until smooth. Gradually beat in the chocolate mixture. Sift the flour into the chocolate mixture. Add the pecans and the white and milk chocolate and gently fold in until mixed thoroughly.

Spoon the mixture into the prepared tin and level the top. Bake on the centre shelf of the preheated oven for 45 minutes, or until just firm to the touch in the centre and crusty on top. Leave to cool in the tin, then turn out onto a wire rack. Trim off the crusty edges and cut into 15 squares. Store in an airtight container.

Try this: FOR AN ALTERNATIVE: 168   FOR KIDS: 172

Pecan Caramel Millionaire's Shortbread

MAKES 20

125 g/4 oz butter, softened
2 tbsp smooth peanut butter
75 g/3 oz caster sugar
75 g/3 oz cornflour
175 g/6 oz plain flour

For the filling:
200 g/7 oz caster sugar
125 g/4 oz butter
2 tbsp golden syrup
75 g/3 oz liquid glucose
75 ml/3 fl oz water
400 g can sweetened

condensed milk
175 g/6 oz pecans,
    roughly chopped
For the topping:
75 g/3 oz plain dark
    chocolate
1 tbsp butter

Preheat the oven to 180°C/350°F/Gas Mark 4, 10 minutes before baking. Lightly oil and line an 18 cm x 28 cm/7 x 11 inch tin with greaseproof paper.

Cream together the butter, peanut butter and sugar until light. Sift in the cornflour and flour together and mix in to make a smooth dough. Press the mixture into the prepared tin and prick all over with a fork. Bake in the preheated oven for 20 minutes, until just golden. Remove from the oven.

Meanwhile, for the filling, combine the sugar, butter, golden syrup, glucose, water and milk in a heavy-based saucepan. Stir constantly over a low heat without boiling until the sugar has dissolved. Increase the heat and boil steadily, stirring constantly, for about 10 minutes until the mixture turns a golden caramel colour. Remove the saucepan from the heat and add the pecans. Pour over the shortbread base immediately. Allow to cool, then refrigerate for at least 1 hour.

Break the chocolate into small pieces and put into a heatproof bowl with the butter. Place over a saucepan of barely simmering water, ensuring that the bowl does not come into contact with the water. Leave until melted, then stir together well. Pour the chocolate evenly over the shortbread, spreading thinly to cover. Leave to set, cut into squares and serve.

Try this: FOR AN ALTERNATIVE: 164   FOR KIDS: 38

Chocolate Walnut Squares

MAKES 24

125 g/4 oz butter
150 g/5 oz plain dark
    chocolate, broken
    into squares
450 g/1 lb caster sugar
½ tsp vanilla essence
200 g/7 oz plain flour

75 g/3 oz self-raising flour
50 g/2 oz cocoa powder
225 g/8 oz mayonnaise, at
    room temperature

For the chocolate glaze:
125 g/4 oz plain dark

chocolate, broken
    into squares
40 g/1½ oz unsalted butter
24 walnut halves
1 tbsp icing sugar,
    for dusting

Preheat the oven to 170°C/325°F/Gas Mark 3, 10 minutes before baking. Oil and line a 28 x 18 x 2.5 cm/11 x 7 x 1 inch cake tin with non-stick baking parchment.

Place the butter, chocolate, sugar, vanilla essence and 225 ml/8 fl oz of cold water in a heavy-based saucepan. Heat gently, stirring occasionally, until the chocolate and butter have melted, but do not allow to boil.

Sift the flours and cocoa powder into a large bowl and make a well in the centre. Add the mayonnaise and about one third of the chocolate mixture and beat until smooth. Gradually beat in the remaining chocolate mixture. Pour into the prepared tin and bake on the centre shelf of the preheated oven for 1 hour, or until slightly risen and firm to the touch. Place the tin on a wire rack and leave to cool. Remove the cake from the tin and peel off the parchment.

To make the chocolate glaze, place the chocolate and butter in a small saucepan with 1 tablespoon of water and heat very gently, stirring occasionally until melted and smooth. Leave to cool until the chocolate has thickened, then spread evenly over the cake. Chill the cake in the refrigerator for about 5 minutes, then mark into 24 squares. Lightly dust the walnut halves with a little icing sugar and place one on the top of each square. Cut into pieces and store in an airtight container until ready to serve.

Try this: FOR AN ALTERNATIVE: 150   FOR KIDS: 176

Chunky Chocolate Muffins

MAKES 7

50 g/2 oz plain dark chocolate, roughly chopped
50 g/2 oz light muscovado sugar
25 g/1 oz butter, melted

125 ml/4 fl oz milk, heated to room temperature
½ tsp vanilla essence
1 medium egg, lightly beaten
150 g/5 oz self-raising flour
½ tsp baking powder

pinch of salt
75 g/3 oz white chocolate, chopped
2 tsp icing sugar (optional)

Preheat the oven to 200°C/400°F/Gas Mark 6, 15 minutes before baking. Line a muffin or deep bun tin tray with seven paper muffin cases or oil the individual compartments well.

Place the plain chocolate in a large, heatproof bowl set over a saucepan of very hot water and stir occasionally until melted. Remove the bowl and leave to cool for a few minutes.

Stir the sugar and butter into the melted chocolate, then the milk, vanilla essence and egg. Sift in the flour, baking powder and salt together. Add the chopped white chocolate, then using a metal spoon, fold together quickly, taking care not to over mix.

Divide the mixture between the paper cases, piling it up in the centre. Bake on the centre shelf of the preheated oven for 20–25 minutes, or until well risen and firm to the touch.

Lightly dust the tops of the muffins with icing sugar as soon as they come out of the oven, if using. Leave the muffins in the tins for a few minutes, then transfer to a wire rack. Serve warm or cold.

 Try this: FOR AN ALTERNATIVE: 198   FOR KIDS: 144

Chocolate Madeleines

MAKES 10

125 g/4 oz butter
125 g/4 oz soft light
    brown sugar
2 medium eggs,
    lightly beaten
1 drop almond essence
1 tbsp ground almonds

75 g/3 oz self-raising flour
20 g/¾ oz cocoa powder
1 tsp baking powder

To finish:
5 tbsp apricot conserve
1 tbsp amaretto liqueur,

brandy or orange juice
50 g/2 oz desiccated coconut
10 large chocolate buttons
    (optional)

Preheat the oven to 180°C/350°F/Gas Mark 4, 10 minutes before baking. Lightly oil 10 dariole moulds and line the bases of each with a small circle of non-stick baking parchment. Stand the moulds on a baking tray.

Cream the butter and sugar together until light and fluffy. Gradually add the eggs, beating well between each addition. Beat in the almond essence and ground almonds.

Sift the flour, cocoa powder and baking powder over the creamed mixture. Gently fold in using a metal spoon. Divide the mixture equally between the prepared moulds – each should be about half full.

Bake on the centre shelf of the preheated oven for 20 minutes, or until well risen and firm to the touch. Leave in the tins for a few minutes, then run a small palette knife round the edge and turn out onto a wire rack to cool. Remove the paper circles from the sponges.

Heat the conserve with the liqueur, brandy or juice in a small saucepan. Sieve to remove any lumps. If necessary, trim the sponge bases, so they are flat. Brush the tops and sides with warm conserve, then roll in the coconut. Top each with a chocolate button, fixed by brushing its base with conserve.

Try this: FOR AN ALTERNATIVE: 188   FOR KIDS: 154

Marbled Chocolate & Orange Loaf

CUTS INTO 6 SLICES

50 g/2 oz plain dark
   chocolate, broken
   into squares
125 g/4 oz butter, softened
125 g/4 oz caster sugar

zest of 1 orange
2 medium eggs, beaten
125 g/4 oz self-raising flour
2 tsp orange juice
1 tbsp cocoa powder, sifted

To finish:
1 tbsp icing sugar
1 tsp cocoa powder

Preheat the oven to 180°C/350°F/Gas Mark 4. Lightly oil a 450 g/1 lb loaf tin and line the base with a layer of non-stick baking paper.

Put the chocolate in a bowl over a saucepan of very hot water. Stir occasionally until melted. Remove and leave until just cool, but not starting to reset.

Meanwhile, cream together the butter, sugar and orange zest until pale and fluffy. Gradually add the beaten eggs, beating well after each addition. Sift in the flour, add the orange juice and fold with a metal spoon or rubber spatula. Divide the mixture by half into two separate bowls. Gently fold the cocoa powder and chocolate into one half of the mixture.

Drop tablespoonfuls of each cake mixture into the prepared tin, alternating between the orange and chocolate mixtures. Briefly swirl the colours together with a knife to give a marbled effect.

Bake in the preheated oven for 40 minutes, or until firm and a fine skewer inserted into the centre comes out clean. Leave in the tin for 5 minutes, then turn out and cool on a wire rack. Carefully remove the lining paper.

Dust the cake with the icing sugar and then with the cocoa powder. Cut into thick slices and serve.

Try this: FOR AN ALTERNATIVE: 192   FOR KIDS: 42

Chocolate & Coconut Cake

CUTS INTO 8 SLICES

125 g/4 oz plain dark chocolate, roughly chopped
175 g/6 oz butter or margarine
175 g/6 oz caster sugar
3 medium eggs, beaten

15 g/6 oz self-raising flour
1 tbsp cocoa powder
50 g/2 oz desiccated coconut

For the icing:
125 g/4 oz butter or margarine

2 tbsp creamed coconut
225 g/8 oz icing sugar
25 g/1 oz desiccated coconut, lightly toasted

Preheat the oven to 180°C/350°F/Gas Mark 4, 10 minutes before baking. Melt the chocolate in a small bowl placed over a saucepan of gently simmering water, ensuring that the base of the bowl does not touch the water. When the chocolate has melted, stir until smooth and allow to cool.

Lightly oil and line the bases of two 18 cm/7 inch sandwich tins with greaseproof paper. In a large bowl, beat the butter or margarine and sugar together with a wooden spoon until light and creamy. Beat in the eggs a little at a time, then stir in the melted chocolate.

Sift the flour and cocoa powder together and gently fold into the chocolate mixture with a metal spoon or rubber spatula. Add the desiccated coconut and mix lightly. Divide between the two prepared tins and smooth the tops. Bake in the preheated oven for 25–30 minutes, or until a skewer comes out clean when inserted into the centre of the cake. Allow to cool in the tin for 5 minutes, then turn out, discard the lining paper and leave on a wire rack until cold.

Beat together the butter or margarine and creamed coconut until light. Add the icing sugar and mix well. Spread half of the icing on one cake and press the cakes together. Spread the remaining icing over the top, sprinkle with the coconut and serve.

Try this: FOR AN ALTERNATIVE: 184   FOR KIDS: 196

Double Chocolate Cake with Cinnamon

CUTS INTO 10 SLICES

50 g/2 oz cocoa powder
1 tsp ground cinnamon
225 g/8 oz self-raising flour
225 g/8 oz unsalted butter

or margarine
225 g/8 oz caster sugar
4 large eggs

For the filling:
125 g/4 oz white chocolate
50 ml/2 fl oz double cream
25 g/1 oz plain dark chocolate

Preheat the oven to 190°C/375°F/Gas Mark 5, 10 minutes before baking. Lightly oil and line the base of two 20.5 cm/8 inch sandwich tins with greaseproof or baking paper. Sift the cocoa powder, cinnamon and flour together and reserve.

In a large bowl, cream the butter or margarine and sugar until light and fluffy. Beat in the eggs a little at a time until they are all incorporated and the mixture is smooth. If it looks curdled at any point beat in 1 tablespoon of the sifted flour. Using a rubber spatula or metal spoon, fold the sifted flour and cocoa powder into the egg mixture until mixed well.

Divide between the two prepared cake tins, and level the surface. Bake in the preheated oven for 25–30 minutes, until springy to the touch and a skewer inserted into the centre of the cake comes out clean. Turn out on to a wire rack to cool.

To make the filling, coarsely break the white chocolate and heat the cream very gently in a small saucepan. Add the broken chocolate, stirring until melted. Leave to cool, then using half of the cooled white chocolate sandwich the cakes together.

Top the cake with the remaining cooled white chocolate. Coarsely grate the dark chocolate over the top and serve.

Try this: FOR AN ALTERNATIVE: 48   FOR KIDS: 182

Double Marble Cake

CUTS INTO 8-10 SLICES

75 g/3 oz white chocolate
75 g/3 oz plain
   dark chocolate
175 g/6 oz caster sugar
175 g/6 oz butter
4 medium eggs, separated

125 g/4 oz plain flour, sifted
75 g/3 oz ground almonds

Fot the topping:
50 g/2 oz white chocolate,
   chopped

75 g/3 oz plain dark
   chocolate, chopped
50 ml/2 fl oz double cream
100 g/3½ oz unsalted butter

Preheat the oven to 180°C/350°F/Gas Mark 4, 10 minutes before baking. Lightly oil and line the base of a 20.5 cm/8 inch cake tin. Break the white and dark chocolate into small pieces, then place in two separate bowls placed over two pans of simmering water, ensuring that the bowls are not touching the water. Heat the chocolate until melted and smooth.

In a large bowl, cream the sugar and butter together until light and fluffy. Beat in the egg yolks, one at a time and add a spoonful of flour after each addition. Stir in the ground almonds. In another bowl whisk the egg whites until stiff. Gently fold in the egg whites and the remaining sifted flour alternately into the almond mixture until all the flour and egg whites have been incorporated. Divide the mixture between two bowls. Gently stir the white chocolate into one bowl, then add the dark chocolate to the other bowl.

Place alternating spoonfuls of the chocolate mixtures in the prepared cake tin. Using a skewer, swirl the mixtures together to get a marbled effect, then tap the tin on the work surface to level the mixture. Bake in the preheated oven for 40 minutes, or until cooked through, then leave to cool for 5 minutes in the tin, before turning out onto a wire rack to cool completely.

Melt the chocolate with the cream and butter and stir until smooth. Cool, then whisk until thick and swirl over the top of the cake.

Try this: FOR AN ALTERNATIVE: 186   FOR KIDS: 44

Dark Chocolate Layered Torte

CUTS INTO 10-12 SLICES

175 g/6 oz butter
1 tbsp instant coffee granules
150 g/ 5 oz plain
    dark chocolate
350 g/12 oz caster sugar
150 g/5 oz self-raising flour

125 g/4 oz plain flour
2 tbsp cocoa powder
2 medium eggs
1 tsp vanilla essence
215 g/7½ oz plain dark
    chocolate, melted

125 g/4 oz butter, melted
40 g/1½ oz icing sugar, sifted
2 tsp raspberry jam
2½ tbsp chocolate liqueur
100 g/3½ oz toasted
    flaked almonds

Preheat the oven to 150°C/300°F/Gas Mark 2, 10 minutes before baking. Line a 23 cm/9 inch square cake tin. Melt the butter in a saucepan, remove from the heat and stir in the coffee granules and 225 ml/8 fl oz hot water. Add the plain dark chocolate and sugar and stir until smooth, then pour into a bowl. In another bowl, sift together the flours and cocoa powder. Using an electric whisk, whisk the sifted mixture into the chocolate mixture until smooth. Beat in the eggs and vanilla essence. Pour into the tin and bake in the preheated oven for 1¼ hours or until firm. Leave for at least 5 minutes before turning out onto a wire rack to cool.

Meanwhile, mix together 200 g/7 oz of the melted dark chocolate with the butter and icing sugar and beat until smooth. Leave to cool, then beat again. Reserve 4–5 tablespoons of the chocolate filling. Cut the cooled cake in half to make two rectangles, then split each rectangle in three horizontally. Place one cake layer on a serving plate and spread thinly with the jam, then a thin layer of dark chocolate filling. Top with a second cake layer and sprinkle with a little liqueur, then spread thinly with filling. Repeat with the remaining cake layers, liqueur and filling.

Chill in the refrigerator for 2–3 hours or until firm. Cover the cake with the reserved chocolate filling and press the flaked almonds into the sides of the cake. Place the remaining melted chocolate in a non-stick baking parchment piping bag. Snip a small hole in the tip and pipe thin lines 2 cm/¾ inch apart crossways over the cake. Drag a cocktail stick lengthways through the icing in alternating directions to create a feathered effect on the top. Serve.

Chocolate Mousse Sponge

CUTS INTO 8-10 SLICES

3 medium eggs
75 g/3 oz caster sugar
1 tsp vanilla essence
50 g/2 oz self-raising
    flour, sifted
25 g/1 oz ground almonds
50 g/2 oz plain dark

chocolate, grated
icing sugar, for dusting
freshly sliced strawberries,
    to decorate

For the mousse:
2 sheets gelatine

50 ml/2 fl oz double cream
100 g/3½ oz plain dark
    chocolate, chopped
1 tsp vanilla essence
4 medium egg whites
125 g/4 oz caster sugar

Preheat the oven to 180°C/350°F/Gas Mark 4, 10 minutes before baking. Lightly oil and line a 23 cm/9 inch round cake tin and lightly oil the sides of a 23 cm/9 inch springform tin. Whisk the eggs, sugar and vanilla essence until thick and creamy. Fold in the flour, ground almonds and dark chocolate. Spoon the mixture into the prepared round cake tin and bake in the preheated oven for 25 minutes or until firm. Turn out onto a wire rack to cool.

For the mousse, soak the gelatine in 50 ml/2 fl oz of cold water for 5 minutes until softened. Meanwhile, heat the double cream in a small saucepan, when almost boiling, remove from the heat and stir in the chocolate and vanilla essence. Stir until the chocolate melts. Squeeze the excess water out of the gelatine and add to the chocolate mixture. Stir until dissolved, then pour into a large bowl. Whisk the egg whites until stiff, then gradually add the caster sugar, whisking well between each addition. Fold the egg white mixture into the chocolate mixture in two batches.

Split the cake into two layers. Place one layer in the bottom of the springform tin. Pour in the chocolate mousse mixture, then top with the second layer of cake. Chill in the refrigerator for 4 hours or until the mousse has set. Loosen the sides and remove the cake from the tin. Dust with icing sugar and decorate the top with a few freshly sliced strawberries. Serve cut into slices.

Try this: FOR AN ALTERNATIVE: 282   FOR KIDS: 176

Chocolate Chiffon Cake

CUTS INTO 10-12 SLICES

50 g/2 oz cocoa powder
300 g/11 oz self-raising flour
550 g/1¼ lb caster sugar
7 medium eggs, separated
125 ml/4 fl oz vegetable oil
1 tsp vanilla essence

75 g/3 oz walnuts
50 g/2 oz plain dark
   chocolate
200 g/7 oz plain dark
   chocolate, melted

For the icing:
175 g/6 oz butter
275 g/10 oz icing sugar, sifted
2 tbsp cocoa powder, sifted
2 tbsp brandy

Preheat the oven to 170°C/325°F/Gas Mark 3, 10 minutes before serving. Line a 23 cm/ 9 inch round cake tin. Lightly oil a baking sheet. Blend the cocoa powder with 175 ml/6 fl oz boiling water and leave to cool. Place the flour and 350 g/12 oz of the caster sugar in a large bowl, and add the cocoa mixture, egg yolks, oil and vanilla essence. Whisk until smooth and lighter in colour. Whisk the egg whites in a clean, grease-free bowl until soft peaks form, then fold into the cocoa mixture. Pour into the prepared tin and bake in the preheated oven for 1 hour or until firm. Leave for 5 minutes before turning out onto a wire rack to cool.

To make the icing, cream together 125 g/4 oz of the butter with the icing sugar, cocoa powder and brandy until smooth, then reserve. Melt the remaining butter and blend with 150 g/5 oz of the melted dark chocolate. Stir until smooth and then leave until thickened. Place the remaining caster sugar into a heavy-based saucepan over a low heat and heat until the sugar has melted and is a deep golden brown. Add the walnuts and the remaining melted chocolate to the melted sugar and pour onto the prepared baking sheet. Leave until cold and brittle, then chop finely. Reserve.

Split the cake into three layers, place one layer onto a serving plate and spread with half of the brandy butter icing. Top with a second cake layer and spread with the remaining brandy butter icing. Arrange the third cake layer on top. Cover the cake with the thickened chocolate glaze. Sprinkle with the walnut praline and serve.

Try this: FOR AN ALTERNATIVE: 194 FOR KIDS: 60

White Chocolate & Passion Fruit Cake

CUTS INTO 8-10 SLICES

125 g/4 oz white chocolate
125 g/4 oz butter
225 g/8 oz caster sugar
2 medium eggs
125 ml/4 fl oz soured cream
200 g/7 oz plain flour, sifted

75 g/3 oz self-raising
    flour, sifted
125 g/4 oz white chocolate,
    coarsely grated, to decorate

For the icing:
200 g/7 oz caster sugar
4 tbsp passion fruit juice
    (about 8–10 fruits, sieved)
1½ tbsp passion fruit seeds
250 g/9 oz unsalted butter

Preheat the oven to 180°C/350°F/Gas Mark 4, 10 minutes before baking. Lightly oil and line two 20.5 cm/8 inch cake tins. Melt the white chocolate in a heatproof bowl set over a saucepan of simmering water. Stir in 125 ml/4 fl oz warm water and stir, then leave to cool. Whisk the butter and sugar together until light and fluffy, add the eggs, one at a time, beating well after each addition. Beat in the chocolate mixture, soured cream and sifted flours. Divide the mixture into eight portions. Spread one portion into each of the tins. Bake in the preheated oven for 10 minutes, or until firm, then turn out onto wire racks. Repeat with the remaining mixture to make eight cake layers.

To make the icing, place 125 ml/4 fl oz of water with 50 g/2 oz of the sugar in a saucepan. Heat gently, stirring, until the sugar has dissolved. Bring to the boil and simmer for 2 minutes. Remove from the heat and cool, then add 2 tablespoons of the passion fruit juice. Reserve. Blend the remaining sugar with 50 ml/2 fl oz of water in a small saucepan and stir constantly over a low heat, without boiling, until the sugar has dissolved. Remove from the heat and cool. Stir in the remaining passion fruit juice and the seeds. Cool, then strain. Using an electric whisk, beat the butter in a bowl until very pale. Gradually beat in the syrup.

Place one layer of cake on a serving plate. Brush with the syrup and spread with a thin layer of icing. Repeat with the remaining cake, syrup and icing. Cover the cake with the remaining icing. Press the chocolate curls into the top and sides to decorate and serve.

Sachertorte

CUTS INTO 10-12 SLICES

150 g/5 oz plain
  dark chocolate
150 g/5 oz unsalted
  butter, softened
125 g/4 oz caster sugar,

plus 2 tbsp
3 medium eggs, separated
150 g/5 oz plain flour, sifted
To decorate:
225 g/8 oz apricot jam

125 g/4 oz plain dark
  chocolate, chopped
125 g/4 oz unsalted butter
25 g/1 oz milk chocolate

Preheat the oven to 180°C/350°F/Gas Mark 4, 10 minutes before baking. Lightly oil and line a deep 23 cm/9 inch cake tin. Melt the 150 g/5 oz of chocolate in a heatproof bowl set over a saucepan of simmering water. Stir in 1 tablespoon of water and leave to cool. Beat the butter and 125 g/4 oz of the sugar together until light and fluffy. Beat in the egg yolks, one at a time, beating well between each addition. Stir in the melted chocolate, then the flour.

In a clean, grease-free bowl, whisk the egg whites until stiff peaks form, then whisk in the remaining sugar. Fold into the chocolate mixture and spoon into the prepared tin. Bake in the pre-heated oven for 30 minutes until firm. Leave for 5 minutes, then turn out onto a wire rack to cool. Leave the cake upside down.

To decorate the cake, split the cold cake in two and place one half on a serving plate. Heat the jam and rub through a fine sieve. Brush half the jam onto the first cake half, then cover with the remaining cake layer and brush with the remaining jam. Leave at room temperature for 1 hour or until the jam has set.

Place the plain dark chocolate with the butter into a heatproof bowl set over a saucepan of simmering water and heat until the chocolate has melted. Stir occasionally until smooth, then leave until thickened. Use to cover the cake. Melt the milk chocolate in a heatproof bowl set over a saucepan of simmering water. Place in a small greaseproof piping bag and snip a small hole at the tip. Pipe 'Sache'r with a large 'S' on the top. Leave to set at room temperature.

Try this: FOR AN ALTERNATIVE: 194 FOR KIDS: 164

Whole Orange & Chocolate Cake With Marmalade Cream

CUTS 6-8 SLICES

1 small orange, scrubbed
2 medium eggs, separated,
    plus 1 whole egg
150 g/5 oz caster sugar
125 g/4 oz ground almonds

75 g/3 oz plain dark
    chocolate, melted
100 ml/3½ fl oz
    double cream
200 g/7 oz full fat soft cheese

25 g/1 oz icing sugar
2 tbsp orange marmalade
orange zest, to decorate

Preheat the oven to 180°C/350°F/Gas Mark 4, 10 minutes before baking. Lightly oil and line the base of a 900 g/2 lb loaf tin. Place the orange in a small saucepan, cover with cold water and bring to the boil. Simmer for 1 hour until completely soft. Drain and leave to cool.

Place 2 egg yolks, 1 whole egg and the sugar in a heatproof bowl set over a saucepan of simmering water and whisk until doubled in bulk. Remove from the heat and continue to whisk for 5 minutes until cooled. Cut the whole orange in half and discard the seeds, then place into a food processor or blender and blend to a purée. Carefully fold the purée into the egg yolk mixture with the ground almonds and melted chocolate. Whisk the egg whites until stiff peaks form. Fold a large spoonful of the egg whites into the chocolate mixture, then gently fold the remaining egg whites into the mixture.

Pour into the prepared tin and bake in the preheated oven for 50 minutes, or until firm and a skewer inserted into the centre comes out clean. Cool in the tin before turning out of the tin and carefully discarding the lining paper.

Meanwhile, whip the double cream until just thickened. In another bowl, blend the soft cheese with the icing sugar and marmalade until smooth, then fold in the double cream. Chill the marmalade cream in the refrigerator until required. Decorate with orange zest and serve the cake cut in slices with the marmalade cream.

Try this: FOR AN ALTERNATIVE: 68   FOR KIDS: 44

Cranberry & White Chocolate Cake

SERVES 4

225 g/8 oz butter, softened
250 g/9 oz full fat soft cheese
150 g/5 oz light soft
   brown sugar
200 g/7 oz caster sugar

grated zest of ½ orange
1 tsp vanilla essence
4 medium eggs
375 g/13 oz plain flour
2 tsp baking powder

200 g/7 oz cranberries,
   thawed if frozen
225 g/8 oz white chocolate,
   coarsely chopped
2 tbsp orange juice

Preheat the oven to 180°C/350°F/Gas Mark 4, 10 minutes before baking. Lightly oil and flour a 23 cm/9 inch kugelhopf tin or ring tin.

Using an electric mixer, cream the butter and cheese with the sugars until light and fluffy. Add the grated orange zest and vanilla essence and beat until smooth, then beat in the eggs, one at a time.

Sift the flour and baking powder together and stir into the creamed mixture, beating well after each addition. Fold in the cranberries and 175 g/6 oz of the white chocolate. Spoon into the prepared tin and bake in the preheated oven for 1 hour, or until firm and a skewer inserted into the centre comes out clean. Cool in the tin before turning out onto on a wire rack.

Melt the remaining white chocolate, stir until smooth, then stir in the orange juice and leave to cool until thickened. Transfer the cake to a serving plate and spoon over the white chocolate and orange glaze. Leave to set.

Try this: FOR AN ALTERNATIVE: 282 FOR KIDS: 168

Chocolate Brioche Bake

SERVES 6

200 g/7 oz plain dark chocolate, broken into pieces
75 g/3 oz unsalted butter
225 g/8 oz brioche, sliced

1 tsp pure orange oil or 1 tbsp grated orange rind
½ tsp freshly grated nutmeg
3 medium eggs, beaten
25 g/1 oz golden

caster sugar
600 ml/1 pint milk
cocoa powder and icing sugar for dusting

Preheat the oven to 180°C/350°F/Gas Mark 4, 10 minutes before baking. Lightly oil or butter a 1.7 litre/3 pint ovenproof dish. Melt the chocolate with 25 g/1 oz of the butter in a heatproof bowl set over a saucepan of simmering water. Stir until smooth.

Arrange half of the sliced brioche in the ovenproof dish, overlapping the slices slightly, then pour over half of the melted chocolate. Repeat the layers, finishing with a layer of chocolate.

Melt the remaining butter in a saucepan. Remove from the heat and stir in the orange oil or rind, the nutmeg and the beaten eggs. Continuing to stir, add the sugar and finally the milk. Beat thoroughly and pour over the brioche. Leave to stand for 30 minutes before baking.

Bake on the centre shelf in the preheated oven for 45 minutes, or until the custard is set and the topping is golden brown. Leave to stand for 5 minutes, then dust with cocoa powder and icing sugar. Serve warm.

Try this: FOR AN ALTERNATIVE: 234   FOR KIDS: 90

Individual Steamed Chocolate Puddings

SERVES 8

150 g/5 oz unsalted
  butter, softened
175 g/6 oz light
  muscovado sugar
½ tsp freshly grated nutmeg

25 g/1 oz plain white flour, sifted
4 tbsp cocoa powder, sifted
5 medium eggs, separated
125 g/4 oz ground almonds
50 g/2 oz white breadcrumbs

To serve:
Greek yogurt
orange-flavoured
  chocolate curls

Preheat the oven to 180°C/350°F/Gas Mark 4, 10 minutes before baking. Lightly oil and line the bases of eight individual 175 ml/6 fl oz pudding basins with a small circle of non-stick baking parchment.

Cream the butter with 50 g/2 oz of the sugar and the nutmeg until light and fluffy. Sift the flour and cocoa powder together, then stir into the creamed mixture. Beat in the egg yolks and mix well, then fold in the ground almonds and the breadcrumbs.

Whisk the egg whites in a clean, grease-free bowl until stiff and standing in peaks then gradually whisk in the remaining sugar. Using a metal spoon, fold a quarter of the egg whites into the chocolate mixture and mix well, then fold in the remaining egg whites.

Spoon the mixture into the prepared basins, filling them two thirds full to allow for expansion. Cover with a double sheet of tinfoil and secure tightly with string. Stand the pudding basins in a roasting tin and pour in sufficient water to come halfway up the sides of the basins.

Bake in the centre of the preheated oven for 30 minutes, or until the puddings are firm to the touch. Remove from the oven, loosen around the edges and invert onto warmed serving plates. Serve immediately with Greek yogurt and chocolate curls.

Try this: FOR AN ALTERNATIVE: 226 FOR KIDS: 108

White Chocolate Trifle

SERVES 6

1 homemade or bought
    chocolate Swiss roll, sliced
4 tbsp brandy
2 tbsp Irish cream liqueur
425 g can black cherries,
    drained and pitted, with 3

tbsp of the juice reserved
900 ml/1½ pints double cream
125 g/4 oz white chocolate,
    broken into pieces
6 medium egg yolks
50 g/2 oz caster sugar

2 tsp cornflour
1 tsp vanilla essence
50 g/2 oz plain dark
    chocolate, grated
50 g/2 oz milk chocolate,
    grated

Place the Swiss roll slices in the bottom of a trifle dish and pour over the brandy, Irish cream liqueur and a little of the reserved black cherry juice to moisten the Swiss roll. Arrange the black cherries on the top.

Pour 600 ml/1 pint of the cream into a saucepan and add the white chocolate. Heat gently to just below simmering point. Whisk together the egg yolks, caster sugar, cornflour and vanilla essence in a small bowl.

Gradually whisk the egg mixture into the hot cream, then strain into a clean saucepan and return to the heat. Cook the custard gently, stirring throughout until thick and coats the back of a spoon.

Leave the custard to cool slightly, then pour over the trifle. Leave the trifle to chill in the refrigerator for at least 3–4 hours, or preferably overnight.

Before serving, lightly whip the remaining cream until soft peaks form, then spoon the cream over the set custard. Using the back of a spoon, swirl the cream in a decorative pattern. Sprinkle with grated plain and milk chocolate and serve.

Try this: FOR AN ALTERNATIVE: 124   FOR KIDS: 264

Chocolate Pear Pudding

SERVES 6

140 g/4½ oz butter, softened
2 tbsp soft brown sugar
400 g can of pear halves,
   drained and juice
   reserved

25 g/1 oz walnut halves
125 g/4 oz golden caster
   sugar
2 medium eggs, beaten
75 g/3 oz self-raising

flour, sifted
50 g/2 oz cocoa powder
1 tsp baking powder
prepared chocolate custard,
   to serve

Preheat the oven to 190°C/375°F/Gas Mark 5, 10 minutes before baking. Butter a 20.5 cm/ 8 inch sandwich tin with 15 g/½ oz of the butter and sprinkle the base with the soft brown sugar. Arrange the drained pear halves on top of the sugar, cut-side down. Fill the spaces between the pears with the walnut halves, flat-side upwards.

Cream the remaining butter with the caster sugar then gradually beat in the beaten eggs, adding 1 tablespoon of the flour after each addition. When all the eggs have been added, stir in the remaining flour.

Sift the cocoa powder and baking powder together, then stir into the creamed mixture with 1–2 tablespoons of the reserved pear juice to give a smooth dropping consistency.

Spoon the mixture over the pear halves, smoothing the surface. Bake in the preheated oven for 20–25 minutes, or until well risen and the surface springs back when lightly pressed.

Remove from the oven and leave to cool for 5 minutes. Using a palate knife, loosen the sides and invert onto a serving plate. Serve with custard.

Try this: FOR AN ALTERNATIVE: 100   FOR KIDS: 112

Sticky Chocolate Surprise Pudding

SERVES 6-8

150 g/5 oz self-raising flour
25 g/1 oz cocoa powder
200 g/7 oz golden
   caster sugar
75 g/3 oz mint-flavoured
   chocolate, chopped

175 ml/6 fl oz full cream milk
2 tsp vanilla essence
50 g/2 oz unsalted butter,
   melted
1 medium egg
sprig of fresh mint, to decorate

For the sauce:
175 g/6 oz dark muscovado
   sugar
125 g/4 oz cocoa powder
600 ml/1 pint very hot water

Preheat the oven to 180°C/350°F/Gas Mark 4, 10 minutes before baking. Lightly oil a 1.4 litre/2½ pint ovenproof soufflé dish. Sift the flour and cocoa powder into a large bowl and stir in the caster sugar and the chopped mint-flavoured chocolate and make a well in the centre.

Whisk the milk, vanilla essence and the melted butter together, then beat in the egg. Pour into the well in the dry ingredients and gradually mix together, drawing the dry ingredients in from the sides of the bowl. Beat well until mixed thoroughly. Spoon into the prepared soufflé dish.

To make the sauce, blend the dark muscovado sugar and the cocoa powder together and spoon over the top of the pudding. Carefully pour the hot water over the top of the pudding, but do not mix.

Bake in the preheated oven for 35–40 minutes, or until firm to the touch and the mixture has formed a sauce underneath. Decorate with mint and serve immediately.

Try this: FOR AN ALTERNATIVE: 210   FOR KIDS: 94

White Chocolate Eclairs

SERVES 4-6

50 g/2 oz unsalted butter	6 ripe passion fruit	1 tbsp icing sugar
60 g/2½ oz plain flour, sifted	300 ml/½ pint double cream	125 g/4 oz white chocolate,
2 medium eggs, lightly beaten	3 tbsp kirsch	broken into pieces

Preheat the oven to 190°C/375°F/Gas Mark 5, 10 minutes before baking. Lightly oil a baking sheet. Place the butter and 150 ml/¼ pint of water in a saucepan and heat until the butter has melted, then bring to the boil. Remove the saucepan from the heat and immediately add the flour all at once, beating with a wooden spoon until the mixture forms a ball in the centre of the saucepan. Leave to cool for 3 minutes. Add the eggs a little at a time, beating well after each addition until the paste is smooth, shiny and of a piping consistency.

Spoon the mixture into a piping bag fitted with a plain nozzle. Sprinkle the oiled baking sheet with water. Pipe the mixture onto the baking sheet in 7.5 cm/3 inch lengths, using a knife to cut each pastry length neatly.

Bake in the preheated oven for 18–20 minutes, or until well risen and golden. Make a slit along the side of each eclair, to let the steam escape. Return the eclairs to the oven for a further 2 minutes to dry out. Transfer to a wire rack and leave to cool.

Halve the passion fruit, and using a small spoon, scoop the pulp of four of the fruits into a bowl. Add the cream, kirsch and icing sugar and whip until the cream holds it shape. Carefully spoon or pipe into the eclairs.

Melt the chocolate in a small heatproof bowl set over a saucepan of simmering water and stir until smooth. Leave the chocolate to cool slightly, then spread over the top of the eclairs. Scoop the seeds and pulp out of the remaining passion fruit. Sieve. Use the juice to drizzle around the eclairs when serving.

Try this: FOR AN ALTERNATIVE: 288   FOR KIDS: 280

Chocolate Roulade

SERVES 8

150 g/5 oz golden caster sugar	For the filling:	coconut, chilled
5 medium eggs, separated	300 ml/½ pint double cream	2 tbsp icing sugar
50 g/2 oz cocoa powder	3 tbsp whisky	coarsely shredded
	50 g/2 oz creamed	coconut, toasted

Preheat the oven to 180°C/350°F/Gas Mark 4, 10 minutes before baking. Oil and line a 33 x 23 cm/13 x 9 inch Swiss roll tin with a single sheet of non-stick baking parchment. Dust a large sheet of baking parchment with 2 tablespoons if the caster sugar.

Place the egg yolks in a bowl with the remaining sugar, set over a saucepan of gently simmering water and whisk until pale and thick. Sift the cocoa powder into the mixture and carefully fold in.

Whisk the egg whites in a clean, grease-free bowl until soft peaks form. Gently add 1 tablespoon of the whisked egg whites into the chocolate mixture then fold in the remaining whites. Spoon the mixture onto the prepared tin, smoothing the mixture into the corners. Bake in the preheated oven for 20–25 minutes, or until risen and springy to the touch.

Turn the cooked roulade out onto the sugar-dusted baking parchment and carefully peel off the lining paper. Cover with a clean damp tea towel and leave to cool.

To make the filling, pour the cream and whisky into a bowl and whisk until the cream holds its shape. Grate in the chilled creamed coconut, add the icing sugar and gently stir in. Uncover the roulade and spoon about three quarters of coconut cream on the roulade and roll up. Spoon the remaining cream on the top and sprinkle with the coconut, then serve.

Try this: FOR AN ALTERNATIVE: 82 FOR KIDS: 340

Chocolate Pancakes

SERVES 6

For the pancakes:
75 g/3 oz plain flour
1 tbsp cocoa powder
1 tsp caster sugar
½ tsp freshly grated nutmeg
2 medium eggs
175 ml/6 fl oz milk

75 g/3 oz unsalted butter, melted
For the mango sauce:
1 ripe mango, peeled
  and diced
50 ml/2 fl oz white wine
2 tbsp golden caster sugar
2 tbsp rum

For the filling:
225 g/8 oz plain dark
  chocolate
75 ml/3 fl oz double cream
3 eggs, separated
25 g/1 oz golden
  caster sugar

Preheat the oven to 200°C/400°F/Gas Mark 6, 15 minutes before cooking. To make the pancakes, sift the flour, cocoa powder, sugar and nutmeg into a bowl and make a well in the centre. Beat the eggs and milk together, then gradually beat into the flour mixture to form a batter. Stir in 50 g/2 oz of the melted butter and leave to stand for 1 hour. Heat an 18 cm/7 inch non-stick frying pan and brush with a little melted butter. Add about 3 tablespoons of the batter and swirl to cover the base of the pan. Cook over a medium heat for 1–2 minutes, flip over and cook for a further 40 seconds. Repeat with the remaining batter. Stack the pancakes, interleaving with greaseproof paper.

To make the sauce, place the mango, white wine and sugar in a saucepan and bring to the boil over a medium heat, then simmer for 2–3 minutes, stirring constantly. When the mixture has thickened add the rum. Chill in the refrigerator. For the filling, melt the chocolate and cream in a small, heavy-based saucepan over a medium heat. Stir until smooth, then leave to cool.

Beat the egg yolks with the caster sugar for 3–5 minutes, or until the mixture is pale and creamy, then beat in the chocolate mixture. Beat the egg whites until stiff, then add a little to the chocolate mixture. Stir in the remainder. Spoon a little of the mixture onto a pancake. Fold in half, then fold in half again, forming a triangle. Repeat with the remaining pancakes. Brush the pancakes with a little melted butter and bake in the preheated oven for 15–20 minutes or until the filling is set. Serve hot or cold with the mango sauce.

Try this: FOR AN ALTERNATIVE: 274   FOR KIDS: 240

Triple Chocolate Cheesecake

SERVES 6

For the base:
150 g/5 oz digestive
   biscuits, crushed
50 g/2 oz butter, melted

For the cheesecake:
75 g/3 oz white chocolate,
   roughly chopped
300 ml/½ pint double cream
50 g/2 oz caster sugar
3 medium eggs, beaten
400 g/14 oz full fat soft
   cream cheese
2 tbsp cornflour

75 g/3 oz plain dark
   chocolate, roughly
   chopped
75 g/3 oz milk chocolate,
   roughly chopped
fromage frais,
   to serve

Preheat the oven to 180°C/350°F/Gas Mark 4, 10 minutes before baking. Lightly oil a 23 x 7.5 cm/9 x 3 inch springform tin.

To make the base, mix together the crushed biscuits and melted butter. Press into the base of the tin and leave to set. Chill in the refrigerator.

Place the white chocolate and cream in a small, heavy-based saucepan and heat gently until the chocolate has melted. Stir until smooth and reserve. Beat the sugar and eggs together until light and creamy in colour, add the cream cheese and beat until the mixture is smooth and free from lumps. Stir the reserved white chocolate cream together with the cornflour into the soft cream cheese mixture.

Add the dark and milk chocolate to the soft cream cheese mixture and mix lightly together until blended. Spoon over the chilled base, place on a baking sheet and bake in the preheated oven for 1 hour.

Switch off the heat, open the oven door and leave the cheesecake to cool in the oven. Chill in the refrigerator for at least 6 hours before removing the cheesecake from the tin. Cut into slices and transfer to serving plates. Serve with fromage frais.

Try this: FOR AN ALTERNATIVE: 308   FOR KIDS: 132

Fruity Chocolate Puddings with Sticky Chocolate Sauce

SERVES 4

125 g/4 oz dark
   muscovado sugar
1 orange, peeled and
   segmented
75 g/3 oz cranberries, fresh
   or thawed if frozen
125g/4 oz soft margarine

2 medium eggs
75 g/3 oz plain flour
½ tsp baking powder
3 tbsp cocoa powder
chocolate curls,
   to decorate

For the sticky chocolate sauce:
175 g/6 oz plain dark
   chocolate, broken into pieces
50 g/2 oz butter
50 g/2 oz caster sugar
2 tbsp golden syrup
200 ml/7 fl oz milk

Lightly oil four 200 ml/7 fl oz individual pudding basins and sprinkle with a little of the muscovado sugar. Place a few orange segments in each basin followed by a spoonful of the cranberries. Cream the remaining muscovado sugar with the margarine until light and fluffy, then gradually beat in the eggs a little at a time, adding 1 tablespoon of the flour after each addition. Sift the remaining flour, baking powder and cocoa powder together, then stir into the creamed mixture with 1 tablespoon of cooled boiled water to give a soft dropping consistency. Spoon the mixture into the basins.

Cover each pudding with a double sheet of non-stick baking parchment with a pleat in the centre and secure tightly with string. Cover with a double sheet of tinfoil. Place in the top of a steamer, set over a saucepan of gently simmering water and steam steadily for 45 minutes, or until firm to the touch. Remember to replenish the water if necessary. Remove the puddings from the steamer and leave to rest for about 5 minutes before running a knife around the edges of the puddings and turning out onto individual plates.

Meanwhile, make the chocolate sauce. Melt the chocolate and butter in a heatproof bowl set over a saucepan of gently simmering water. Add the sugar and golden syrup and stir until dissolved, then stir in the milk and continue to cook, stirring often, until the sauce thickens. Decorate the puddings with a few chocolate curls and serve with the sauce.

Try this: FOR AN ALTERNATIVE: 108   FOR KIDS: 316

Chocolate Mallow Pie

SERVES 6

200 g/7 oz digestive biscuits
75 g/3 oz butter, melted
175 g/6 oz plain

dark chocolate
20 marshmallows
1 medium egg, separated

300 ml/½ pint double cream

Place the biscuits in a polythene bag and finely crush with a rolling pin. Alternatively, place in a food processor and blend until fine crumbs are formed.

Melt the butter in a medium-sized saucepan, add the crushed biscuits and mix together. Press into the base of the prepared tin and leave to cool in the refrigerator.

Melt 125 g/4 oz of the chocolate with the marshmallows and 2 tablespoons of water in a saucepan over a gentle heat, stirring constantly. Leave to cool slightly, then stir in the egg yolk, beat well, then return to the refrigerator until cool.

Whisk the egg white until stiff and standing in peaks, then fold into the chocolate mixture. Lightly whip the cream and fold three quarters of it into the chocolate mixture. Reserve the remainder. Spoon the chocolate cream into the flan case and chill in the refrigerator until set.

When ready to serve, spoon the remaining cream over the chocolate pie, swirling in a decorative pattern. Grate the remaining dark chocolate and sprinkle over the cream, then serve.

Try this: FOR AN ALTERNATIVE: 92   FOR KIDS: 120

Chocolate Sponge Pudding with Fudge Sauce

SERVES 4

75 g/3 oz butter
75 g/3 oz caster sugar
50 g/2 oz plain dark
  chocolate, melted
50 g/2 oz self-raising flour
25 g/1 oz drinking chocolate

1 large egg
1 tbsp icing sugar, to dust
crème fraîche, to serve

For the fudge sauce:
50 g/2 oz soft light brown sugar

1 tbsp cocoa powder
40 g/1½ oz pecan nuts,
  roughly chopped
25 g/1 oz caster sugar
300 ml/½ pint hot, strong
  black coffee

Preheat the oven to 170°C/ 325°F/Gas Mark 3. Oil a 900 ml/1½ pint pie dish.

Cream the butter and the sugar together in a large bowl until light and fluffy. Stir in the melted chocolate, flour, drinking chocolate and egg and mix together. Turn the mixture into the prepared dish and level the surface.

To make the fudge sauce, blend the brown sugar, cocoa powder and pecan nuts together and sprinkle evenly over the top of the pudding.

Stir the caster sugar into the hot black coffee until it has dissolved. Carefully pour the coffee over the top of the pudding.

Bake in the preheated oven for 50–60 minutes, until the top is firm to touch. There will now be a rich sauce underneath the sponge. Remove from the oven, dust with icing sugar and serve hot with crème fraîche.

Try this: FOR AN ALTERNATIVE: 314   FOR KIDS: 310

Chocolate Pecan Pie

CUTS INTO 8-10 SLICES

225 g/8 oz shop-bought shortcrust pastry
200 g/7 oz pecan halves
125 g/4 oz plain dark chocolate, chopped
25 g/1 oz butter, diced
3 medium eggs
125 g/4 oz light brown sugar
175 ml/6 fl oz golden syrup
2 tsp vanilla essence
vanilla ice cream, to serve

Preheat the oven to 180°C/350°F/Gas Mark 4, 10 minutes before baking. Roll the prepared pastry out on a lightly floured surface and use to line a 25.5 cm/10 inch pie plate. Roll the trimmings out and use to make a decorative edge around the pie, then chill in the refrigerator for 1 hour.

Reserve about 60 perfect pecan halves, or enough to cover the top of the pie, then coarsely chop the remainder and reserve. Melt the chocolate and butter in a small saucepan over a low heat or in the microwave and reserve.

Beat the eggs and brush the base and sides of the pastry with a little of the beaten egg. Beat the sugar, golden syrup and vanilla essence into the beaten eggs. Add the pecans, then beat in the chocolate mixture.

Pour the filling into the pastry case and arrange the reserved pecan halves in concentric circles over the top. Bake in the preheated oven for 45–55 minutes, or until the filling is well risen and just set. If the pastry edge begins to brown too quickly, cover with strips of tinfoil. Remove from the oven and serve with ice cream.

Try this: FOR AN ALTERNATIVE: 304   FOR KIDS: 236

Fruity Chocolate Bread Pudding

SERVES 4

175 g/6 oz plain dark
  chocolate
1 small fruit loaf
125 g/4 oz ready-to-eat dried

apricots, roughly chopped
450 ml/¾ pint single cream
300 ml/½ pint milk
1 tbsp caster sugar

3 medium eggs
3 tbsp demerara sugar,
  for sprinkling

Preheat the oven to 180˚C/350˚F/Gas Mark 4, 10 minutes before cooking. Lightly butter a shallow ovenproof dish. Break the chocolate into small pieces, then place in a heatproof bowl set over a saucepan of gently simmering water. Heat gently, stirring frequently, until the chocolate has melted and is smooth. Remove from the heat and leave for about 10 minutes or until the chocolate begins to thicken slightly.

Cut the fruit loaf into medium to thick slices, then spread with the melted chocolate. Leave until almost set, then cut each slice in half to form a triangle. Layer the chocolate-coated bread slices and the chopped apricots in the buttered ovenproof dish.

Stir the cream and the milk together, then stir in the caster sugar. Beat the eggs, then gradually beat in the cream and milk mixture. Beat thoroughly until well blended. Carefully pour over the bread slices and apricots and leave to stand for 30 minutes.

Sprinkle with the demerara sugar and place in a roasting tin half filled with boiling water. Cook in the preheated oven for 45 minutes, or until golden and the custard is lightly set. Serve immediately.

Try this: FOR AN ALTERNATIVE: 208   FOR KIDS: 90

French Chocolate Pecan Torte

CUTS INTO 16 SLICES

200 g/7 oz plain dark
  chocolate, chopped
150 g/5 oz butter, diced
4 large eggs
100 g/3½ oz caster sugar
2 tsp vanilla essence

125 g/4 oz pecans,
  finely ground
2 tsp ground cinnamon
24 pecan halves,
  lightly toasted,
  to decorate

For the chocolate glaze:
125 g/4 oz plain dark
  chocolate, chopped
60 g/2½ oz butter, diced
2 tbsp clear honey
¼ tsp ground cinnamon

Preheat the oven to 180°C/350°F/Gas Mark 4, 10 minutes before baking. Lightly butter and line a 20.5 x 5 cm/8 x 2 inch springform tin with non-stick baking paper. Wrap the tin in a large sheet of tinfoil to prevent water seeping in.

Melt the chocolate and butter in a saucepan over a low heat and stir until smooth. Remove from the heat and cool. Using an electric whisk, beat the eggs, sugar and vanilla essence until light and foamy. Gradually beat in the melted chocolate, ground nuts and cinnamon, then pour into the prepared tin.

Set the foil-wrapped tin in a large roasting tin and pour in enough boiling water to come 2 cm/¾ inches up the sides of the tin. Bake in the preheated oven until the edge is set, but the centre is still soft when the tin is gently shaken. Remove from the oven and place on a wire rack to cool.

For the glaze, melt all the ingredients over a low heat until melted and smooth, then remove from the heat. Dip each pecan halfway into the glaze and set on a sheet of non-stick baking paper until set. Allow the remaining glaze to thicken slightly. Remove the cake from the tin and invert. Pour the glaze over the cake smoothing the top and spreading the glaze around the sides. Arrange the glazed pecans around the edge of the torte. Allow to set and serve.

Try this: FOR AN ALTERNATIVE: 296   FOR KIDS: 116

Double Chocolate Truffle Slice

CUTS INTO 12-14 SLICES

1 quantity Chocolate Pastry (see page 302)
300 ml/½ pint double cream
300 g/11 oz plain dark chocolate, chopped
25–40 g/1–1½ oz unsalted butter, diced
50 ml/2 fl oz brandy or liqueur
icing sugar or cocoa powder for dusting

Preheat the oven to 200°C/400°F/Gas Mark 6, 15 minutes before baking. Prepare the chocolate pastry and chill in the refrigerator, according to the instructions.

Roll the dough out to a rectangle about 38 x 15 cm/15 x 6 inches and use to line a rectangular loose-based flan tin. Trim, then chill in the refrigerator for 1 hour.

Place a sheet of non-stick baking parchment and baking beans in the pastry case, then bake blind in the preheated oven for 20 minutes. Remove the baking parchment and beans and bake for 10 minutes more. Leave to cool completely.

Bring the cream to the boil. Remove from the heat and add the chocolate all at once, stirring until melted and smooth. Beat in the butter, then stir in the brandy liqueur. Leave to cool slightly, then pour into the cooked pastry shell. Refrigerate until set.

Cut out 2.5 cm/1 inch strips of non-stick baking parchment. Place over the tart in a criss-cross pattern and dust with icing sugar or cocoa.

Arrange chocolate leaves or curls around the edges of the tart. Refrigerate until ready to serve. Leave to soften at room temperature for 15 minutes before serving.

Try this: FOR AN ALTERNATIVE: 334 FOR KIDS: 332

Double Chocolate Banoffee Tart

CUTS INTO 8 SLICES

2 x 400 g cans sweetened
   condensed milk
175 g/6 oz plain dark
   chocolate, chopped
600 ml/1 pint
   whipping cream
1 tbsp golden syrup

25 g/1 oz butter, diced
150 g/5 oz white chocolate,
   grated or finely chopped
1 tsp vanilla essence
2–3 ripe bananas
cocoa powder,
   for dusting

For the ginger crumb crust:
24–26 gingernut biscuits,
   roughly crushed
100 g/3½ oz butter, melted
1–2 tbsp sugar, or to taste
½ tsp ground ginger

Preheat the oven to 190°C/375°F/Gas Mark 5, 10 minutes before baking. Place the condensed milk in a heavy-based saucepan and place over a gentle heat. Bring to the boil, stirring constantly. Boil gently for about 3–5 minutes or until golden. Remove from the heat and leave to cool. To make the crust, place the biscuits with the melted butter, sugar and ginger in a food processor and blend together. Press into the sides and base of 23 cm/9 inch loose-based flan tin with the back of a spoon. Chill in the refrigerator for 15–20 minutes, then bake in the preheated oven for 5–6 minutes. Remove from the oven and leave to cool.

Melt the dark chocolate in a medium-sized saucepan with 150 ml/¼ pint of the whipping cream, the golden syrup and the butter over a low heat. Stir until smooth. Carefully pour into the crumb crust, tilting the tin to distribute the chocolate layer evenly. Chill in the refrigerator for at least 1 hour or until set. Heat 150 ml/¼ pint of the remaining cream until hot, then add all the white chocolate and stir until melted and smooth. Stir in the vanilla essence and strain into a bowl. Leave to cool to room temperature.

Scrape the cooked condensed milk into a bowl and whisk until smooth. Spread over the chocolate layer, then slice the bananas and arrange evenly over the top. Whisk the remaining cream until soft peaks form. Fold the cream into the white chocolate mixture, then spread over the bananas, swirling to the edge. Dust with cocoa powder and chill until ready to serve.

Chocolate Apricot Linzer Torte

CUTS INTO 10–12 SLICES

For the chocolate
   almond pastry:
75 g/3 oz whole
   blanched almonds
125 g/4 oz caster sugar
215 g/7½ oz plain flour

2 tbsp cocoa powder
1 tsp ground cinnamon
½ tsp salt
grated zest of 1 orange
225 g/8 oz unsalted butter, diced
2–3 tbsp iced water

For the filling:
350 g/12 oz apricot jam
75 g/3 oz milk chocolate,
   chopped
icing sugar, for dusting

Preheat the oven to 375°C/190°F/Gas Mark 5, 10 minutes before baking. Lightly oil a 28 cm/11 inch flan tin. Place the almonds and half the sugar into a food processor and blend until finely ground. Add the remaining sugar, flour, cocoa powder, cinnamon, salt and orange zest and blend again. Add the diced butter and blend in short bursts to form coarse crumbs. Add the water 1 tablespoon at a time until the mixture starts to come together.

Turn onto a lightly floured surface and knead lightly, roll out, then using your fingertips, press half the dough onto the base and sides of the tin. Prick the base with a fork and chill in the refrigerator. Roll out the remaining dough between two pieces of clingfilm to a 28–30.5 cm/11–12 inch round. Slide the round onto a baking sheet and chill in the refrigerator for 30 minutes.

For the filling, spread the apricot jam evenly over the chilled pastry base and sprinkle with the chopped chocolate. Slide the dough round onto a lightly floured surface and peel off the top layer of clingfilm. Using a straight edge, cut the round into 1 cm/½inch strips; allow to soften until slightly flexible. Place half the strips, about 1 cm/½ inch apart, to create a lattice pattern. Press down on each side of each crossing to accentuate the effect. Press the ends of the strips to the edge, cutting off any excess. Bake in the preheated oven for 35 minutes, or until cooked. Leave to cool before dusting with icing sugar and serve cut into slices.

Try this: FOR AN ALTERNATIVE: 100   FOR KIDS: 118

Chocolate Trifle

SERVES 4

1½ homemade or bought
   chocolate Swiss rolls
4 tbsp strawberry jam
3 tbsp medium sherry
3 tbsp brandy
350 g/12 oz fresh strawberries

2 small mangos, peeled,
   stoned and diced
200 g/7 oz plain
   dark chocolate
2 tbsp custard powder
2 tbsp granulated sugar

300 ml/½ pint full fat milk
250 g/9 oz
   mascarpone cheese
300 ml/½ pint double cream
15 g/½ oz toasted flaked
   almonds

Slice the chocolate Swiss roll thickly and spread each slice with a little strawberry jam. Place the Swiss roll slices in the base of a trifle dish or glass bowl. Sprinkle over the sherry and brandy and leave to stand for 10 minutes to let the sherry and brandy soak into the Swiss roll. Slice half the strawberries and scatter evenly over the Swiss roll with half the diced mangos.

Break the chocolate into small pieces and place in a small heatproof bowl set over a saucepan of gently simmering water. Heat gently, stirring occasionally until the chocolate has melted and is smooth and free from lumps.

Blend the custard powder, sugar and milk to a smooth paste in a bowl, then pour into a heavy-based saucepan. Place over a gentle heat and cook, stirring constantly, until the custard is smooth and thick. Add the melted chocolate and stir until smooth and blended. Remove from the heat and leave to cool. Stir in the mascarpone cheese.

Spoon the custard mixture over the fruit and chill in the refrigerator for 1 hour. Whip the cream until soft peaks form and pile over the top of the set custard. Sprinkle over the toasted flaked almonds and decorate with the remaining whole strawberries and diced mango.

Try this: FOR AN ALTERNATIVE: 212 FOR KIDS: 230

Chocolate Brûlée

SERVES 6

175 g/6 oz fresh raspberries
125 g/4 oz caster sugar
5 medium egg yolks

600 ml/1 pint double cream
1 tsp vanilla essence
175 g/6 oz white

chocolate, chopped
6 tbsp demerara sugar

Hull and clean the raspberries. Rinse lightly, then leave to dry on absorbent kitchen paper. Once dry, divide the raspberries evenly between six 150 ml/¼ pint ramekins or individual dishes.

Whisk the caster sugar and egg yolks in a large bowl until very thick. Pour the cream into a heavy-based saucepan, place over a medium-high heat and bring to the boil. Remove from the heat and gradually whisk into the egg mixture, then whisk in the vanilla essence.

Place the bowl over a saucepan of simmering water and cook for about 15–20 minutes, stirring frequently, or until thick and the custard coats the back of a wooden spoon.

Remove the bowl from the heat, add the chopped white chocolate and stir until melted and well blended. Pour over the raspberries in the ramekins and leave to cool. Cover with clingfilm and chill in the refrigerator for 6 hours or until firm.

Preheat the grill. Remove the ramekins from the refrigerator and sprinkle 1 tablespoon of the demerara sugar over each, ensuring that the custard is completely covered.

Cook under the preheated grill for 5–6 minutes, or until the sugar has melted and begun to caramelise. Remove from the grill, leave to cool slightly, then chill again in the refrigerator for at least 1 hour. Serve immediately.

Try this: FOR AN ALTERNATIVE: 130   FOR KIDS: 126

Poached Pears with Chocolate Sauce

SERVES 4

300 ml/½ pint red wine
125 g/4 oz caster sugar
grated rind and juice of 1
   small orange
2 cm/1 inch piece fresh root

ginger, peeled and
   chopped
4 firm pears, such as
   Williams or Conference
175 g/6 oz plain

dark chocolate
150 ml/¼ pint double cream
25 g/1 oz golden
   granulated sugar

Pour the red wine with 150 ml/¼ pint of water into a heavy-based saucepan and stir in the sugar, the orange rind and juice with the ginger. Place over a gentle heat and bring slowly to the boil, stirring occasionally until the sugar has dissolved. Once the sugar has dissolved, boil steadily for 5 minutes, then remove from the heat.

Using a potato peeler, carefully peel the pears, leaving the stalks intact. If preferred, gently remove the cores from the base of each pear. You can, if you prefer, leave the cores intact for a neater finish. If necessary, cut a very thin slice off the base of each pear so they sit upright.

Carefully stand the pears in the hot syrup, return to the heat, cover with a lid and simmer gently for 20 minutes or until tender, turning the pears occasionally. Remove from the heat and leave to cool in the syrup, turning occasionally. Using a slotted spoon, transfer the pears to a large dish.

Strain the syrup, then bring back to the boil and boil rapidly until reduced and syrupy. Add the chocolate, cream and sugar to the saucepan and bring very slowly to the boil, stirring constantly until the chocolate has melted. Arrange the pears on serving plates and carefully spoon over the chocolate sauce. Serve immediately.

Try this: FOR AN ALTERNATIVE: 302   FOR KIDS: 214

Chocolate & Fruit Crumble

SERVES 4

For the crumble:
125 g/4 oz plain flour
125 g/4 oz butter
75 g/3 oz light soft
   brown sugar
50 g/2 oz rolled
   porridge oats
50 g/2 oz hazelnuts, chopped

For the filling:
450 g/1 lb Bramley apples
1 tbsp lemon juice
50 g/2 oz sultanas
50 g/2 oz seedless raisins
50 g/2 oz light soft
   brown sugar
350 g/12 oz pears, peeled,

   cored and chopped
1 tsp ground cinnamon
125 g/4 oz plain
   dark chocolate,
   very roughly chopped
2 tsp caster sugar
   for sprinkling

Preheat the oven to 190°C/375°F/Gas Mark 5, 10 minutes before baking. Lightly oil an ovenproof dish.

For the crumble, sift the flour into a large bowl. Cut the butter into small dice and add to the flour. Rub the butter into the flour until the mixture resembles fine breadcrumbs. Stir the sugar, porridge oats and the chopped hazelnuts into the mixture and reserve.

For the filling, peel the apples, core and slice thickly. Place in a large heavy-based saucepan with the lemon juice and 3 tablespoons of water. Add the sultanas, raisins and the soft brown sugar. Bring slowly to the boil, cover and simmer over a gentle heat for 8–10 minutes, stirring occasionally, or until the apples are slightly softened.

Remove the saucepan from the heat and leave to cool slightly before stirring in the pears, ground cinnamon and the chopped chocolate.

Spoon into the prepared ovenproof dish. Sprinkle the crumble evenly over the top then bake in the preheated oven for 35–40 minutes or until the top is golden. Remove from the oven, sprinkle with the caster sugar and serve immediately.

Try this: FOR AN ALTERNATIVE: 96   FOR KIDS: 88

Chocolate Fruit Tiramisu

SERVES 4

2 ripe passion fruit
2 fresh nectarines
　or peaches
75 g/3 oz sponge
　finger biscuits

125 g/4 oz amaretti biscuits
5 tbsp amaretti liqueur
6 tbsp prepared black coffee
250 g/9 oz mascarpone
　cheese

450 ml/¾ pint fresh custard
200 g/7 oz plain dark
　chocolate, finely chopped
　or grated
2 tbsp cocoa powder, sifted

Cut the passion fruit and scoop out the seeds and reserve. Plunge the nectarines or peaches into boiling water and leave for 2–3 minutes. Carefully remove the nectarines from the water, cut in half and remove the stones. Peel off the skin, chop the flesh finely and reserve.

Break the sponge finger biscuits and amaretti biscuits in half. Place the amaretti liqueur and prepared black coffee into a shallow dish and stir well. Place half the sponge fingers and amaretti biscuits into the amaretti and coffee mixture and soak for 30 seconds. Lift out both biscuits from the liquor and arrange in the bases of four deep, individual glass dishes.

Cream the mascarpone cheese until soft and creamy, then slowly beat in the fresh custard and mix well together. Spoon half the mascarpone mixture over the biscuits in the dishes and sprinkle with 125 g/4 oz of the finely chopped or grated dark chocolate. Arrange half the passion fruit seeds and the chopped nectarine or peaches over the chocolate and sprinkle with half the sifted cocoa powder.

Place the remaining biscuits in the remaining coffee liqueur mixture and soak for 30 seconds, then arrange on top of the fruit and cocoa powder. Top with the remaining chopped or grated chocolate, nectarine or peach and the mascarpone cheese mixture, piling the mascarpone high in the dishes. Chill in the refrigerator for 1½ hours, then spoon the remaining passion fruit seeds and cocoa powder over the desserts. Chill in the refrigerator for 30 minutes and serve.

Try this: FOR AN ALTERNATIVE: 244　FOR KIDS: 258

Orange Chocolate Cheesecake

SERVES 8

225 g/8 oz plain chocolate
    coated digestive biscuits
50 g/2 oz butter
450 g/1 lb mixed fruits, such
    as blueberries and
    raspberries

1 tbsp icing sugar, sifted
few sprigs of fresh mint,
    to decorate

For the filling:
450 g/1 lb soft cream cheese

1 tbsp gelatine
350 g/12 oz orange
    chocolate, broken
    into segments
600 ml/1 pint double cream

Lightly oil and line a 20.5 cm/8 inch round loose-based cake tin with non-stick baking parchment. Place the biscuits in a polythene bag and crush using a rolling pin. Alternatively, use a food processor. Melt the butter in a medium-sized, heavy-based saucepan, add the crushed biscuits and mix well. Press the biscuit mixture into the base of the lined tin, then chill in the refrigerator for 20 minutes.

For the filling, remove the cream cheese from the refrigerator, at least 20 minutes before using, to allow the cheese to come to room temperature. Place the cream cheese in a bowl and beat until smooth, reserve. Pour 4 tablespoons of water into a small bowl and sprinkle over the gelatine. Leave to stand for 5 minutes until spongy. Place the bowl over a saucepan of simmering water and allow to dissolve, stirring occasionally. Leave to cool slightly.

Melt the orange chocolate in a heatproof bowl set over a saucepan of simmering water, then leave to cool slightly. Whip the cream until soft peaks form. Beat the gelatine and chocolate into cream cheese. Fold in the cream. Spoon into the tin and level the surface. Chill in the refrigerator for 4 hours until set.

Remove the cheesecake from the tin and place on a serving plate. Top with the fruits, dust with icing sugar and decorate with sprigs of mint.

Try this: FOR AN ALTERNATIVE: 262   FOR KIDS: 132

White Chocolate Terrine with Red Fruit Compote

SERVES 8

225 g/8 oz white chocolate
300 ml/½ pint double cream
225 g/8 oz full fat soft
    cream cheese

2 tbsp finely grated orange rind
125 g/4 oz caster sugar
350 g/12 oz mixed summer
    fruits, such as

strawberries, blueberries
    and raspberries
1 tbsp Cointreau
sprigs of fresh mint, to decorate

Set the freezer to rapid freeze at least 2 hours before required. Lightly oil and line a 450 g/1 lb loaf tin with clingfilm, taking care to keep the clingfilm as wrinkle free as possible. Break the white chocolate into small pieces and place in a heatproof bowl set over a saucepan of gently simmering water. Leave for 20 minutes or until melted, then remove from the heat and stir until smooth. Leave to cool.

Whip the cream until soft peaks form. Beat the cream cheese until soft and creamy, then beat in the grated orange rind and 50 g/2 oz of the caster sugar. Mix well, then fold in the whipped cream and then the cooled melted white chocolate.

Spoon the mixture into the prepared loaf tin and level the surface. Place in the freezer and freeze for at least 4 hours or until frozen. Once frozen, remember to return the freezer to its normal setting.

Place the fruits with the remaining sugar in a heavy-based saucepan and heat gently, stirring occasionally, until the sugar has dissolved and the juices from the fruits are just beginning to run. Add the Cointreau.

Dip the loaf tin into hot water for 30 seconds and invert onto a serving plate. Carefully remove the tin and clingfilm. Decorate with sprigs of mint and serve sliced with the prepared red fruit compote.

Try this: FOR AN ALTERNATIVE: 218 FOR KIDS: 308

Iced Chocolate & Raspberry Mousse

SERVES 4

12 sponge finger biscuits
juice of 2 oranges
2 tbsp Grand Marnier
300 ml/½ pint double cream
175 g/6 oz plain dark

chocolate, broken into
  small pieces
225 g/8 oz frozen raspberries
6 tbsp icing sugar, sifted
cocoa powder, for dusting

To decorate:
a few fresh whole
  raspberries
few mint leaves
grated white chocolate

Break the sponge finger biscuits into small pieces and divide between four individual glass dishes. Blend together the orange juice and Grand Marnier, then drizzle evenly over the sponge fingers. Cover with clingfilm and chill in the refrigerator for 30 minutes.

Meanwhile, place the cream in a small, heavy-based saucepan and heat gently, stirring occasionally until boiling. Remove the saucepan from the heat then add the pieces of dark chocolate and leave to stand, untouched for about 7 minutes. Using a whisk, whisk the chocolate and cream together, until the chocolate has melted and is well blended and completely smooth. Leave to cool slightly.

Place the frozen raspberries and icing sugar into a food processor or liquidizer and blend until roughly crushed. Fold the crushed raspberries into the cream and chocolate mixture and mix lightly until well blended. Spoon over the chilled sponge finger biscuits.

Lightly dust with a little cocoa powder and decorate with whole raspberries, mint leaves and grated white chocolate. Serve immediately.

Try this: FOR AN ALTERNATIVE: 312   FOR KIDS: 264

Caramelised Chocolate Tartlets

SERVES 6

350 g/12 oz ready-made
shortcrust pastry,
thawed if frozen
150 ml/¼ pint coconut milk
40 g/1½ oz demerara sugar
50 g/2 oz plain dark

chocolate, melted
1 medium egg, beaten
few drops vanilla essence
1 small mango, peeled,
stoned and sliced
1 small papaya, peeled,

deseeded and chopped
1 star fruit, sliced
1 kiwi, peeled and sliced, or
use fruits of your choice

Preheat the oven to 200°C/400°F/Gas Mark 6, 15 minutes before baking. Lightly oil six individual tartlet tins. Roll out the ready-made pastry on a lightly floured surface and use to line the oiled tins. Prick the bases and sides with a fork and line with non-stick baking parchment and baking beans. Bake blind for 10 minutes in the preheated oven, then remove from the oven and discard the baking beans and the baking parchment.

Reduce the oven temperature to 180°C/350°F/Gas Mark 4. Heat the coconut milk and 15 g/ ½ oz of the sugar in a heavy-based saucepan, stirring constantly until the sugar has dissolved. Remove the saucepan from the heat and leave to cool.

Stir the melted chocolate, the beaten egg and the vanilla essence into the cooled coconut milk. Stir until well mixed, then strain into the cooked pastry cases. Place on a baking sheet and bake in the oven for 25 minutes or until set. Remove and leave to cool, then chill in the refrigerator.

Preheat the grill, then arrange the fruits in a decorative pattern on the top of each tartlet. Sprinkle with the remaining demerara sugar and place the tartlets in the grill pan. Grill for 2 minutes or until the sugar bubbles and browns. Turn the tartlets, if necessary and take care not to burn the sugar. Remove from the grill and leave to cool before serving.

Try this: FOR AN ALTERNATIVE: 278   FOR KIDS: 296

Chocolate & Saffron Cheesecake

SERVES 6

¼ tsp saffron threads
175 g/6 oz plain flour
pinch of salt
75 g/3 oz butter
1 tbsp caster sugar
1 medium egg yolk

350 g/12 oz curd cheese
75 g/3 oz golden
   granulated sugar
125 g/4 oz plain dark
   chocolate, melted
   and cooled

6 tbsp milk
3 medium eggs
1 tbsp icing sugar,
   sifted, to decorate

Preheat the oven to 200°C/400°F/Gas Mark 6, 15 minutes before baking. Lightly oil a 20.5 cm/8 inch fluted flan tin. Soak the saffron threads in 1 tablespoon of hot water for 20 minutes. Sift the flour and salt into a bowl. Cut the butter into small cubes, then add to the flour and using your fingertips, rub in the butter until the mixture resembles breadcrumbs. Stir in the sugar. Beat the egg yolk with 1 tablespoon of cold water, add to the mixture and mix together until a smooth and pliable dough is formed. Add a little extra water if necessary. Knead on a lightly floured surface until free from cracks, then wrap in clingfilm and chill in the refrigerator for 30 minutes. Roll the pastry out on a lightly floured surface and use to line the flan tin. Prick the pastry base and sides with a fork and line with non-stick baking parchment and baking beans. Bake blind in the preheated oven for 12 minutes. Remove the beans and baking parchment and continue to bake blind for 5 minutes.

Beat together the curd cheese and granulated sugar, then beat in the melted chocolate, saffron liquid, the milk and eggs, mix until blended thoroughly. Pour the mixture into the cooked flan case and place on a baking sheet. Reduce the oven temperature to 190°C/375°F/Gas Mark 5 and bake for 15 minutes, then reduce the oven temperature to 180°C/350°F/Gas Mark 4 and continue to bake for 20–30 minutes or until set. Remove the cheesecake from the oven and leave for 10 minutes before removing from the flan tin, if serving warm. If serving cold, leave in the flan tin to cool before removing and placing on a serving platter. Sprinkle with icing sugar before serving.

Try this: FOR AN ALTERNATIVE: 254 FOR KIDS: 308

Chocolate Mousse

SERVES 6

175 g/6 oz milk or plain
   chocolate orange
535 g carton ready-
   made custard

450 ml/¾ pint
   double cream
12 Cape gooseberries,
   to decorate

sweet biscuits,
   to serve

Break the chocolate into segments and place in a bowl set over a saucepan of simmering water. Leave until melted, stirring occasionally. Remove the bowl in the pan from the heat and allow the melted chocolate to cool slightly.

Place the custard in a bowl and fold the melted chocolate into it using a metal spoon or rubber spatula. Stir well until completely combined.

Pour the cream into a small bowl and whip until the cream forms soft peaks. Using a metal spoon or rubber spatula, fold in most of the whipped cream into the chocolate mixture.

Spoon into six tall glasses and carefully top with the remaining cream. Leave the desserts to chill in the refrigerator for at least 1 hour or preferably overnight.

Peel back the skins from the gooseberries to form petal shapes and use to decorate the chocolate desserts. Serve with sweet biscuits.

Try this: FOR AN ALTERNATIVE: 258   FOR KIDS: 196

Chocolate Brandy Dream

SERVES 4

175 g/6 oz chocolate, broken
   into pieces
300 ml/½ pint whipping cream

2 tbsp brandy
1 tbsp coffee essence
1 medium egg white

To decorate:
raspberries
blueberries
mint leaves
cocoa powder

Place the pieces of chocolate into a heat-proof bowl placed over a saucepan of gently simmering water and leave to melt slowly, stirring occasionally. Carefully remove the pan and the bowl from the heat and reserve to allow the chocolate to cool.

Pour the cream into a small bowl, whip until soft peaks form, then reserve.

Gently stir the brandy and coffee essence into the chocolate. Mix together gently until blended, then fold in the whipped cream with a metal spoon or rubber spatula.

Briskly whisk the egg white in a small bowl until stiff, then fold into the chocolate mixture with a metal spoon or rubber spatula. Mix the chocolate mixture gently, taking care not to remove the air already whisked into the egg white.

Spoon into four tall glasses and chill for at least 2 hours. Decorate with raspberries, blueberries and mint leaves. Dust with cocoa powder and serve.

Try this: FOR AN ALTERNATIVE: 312 FOR KIDS: 318

White Chocolate & Macadamia Tartlets

MAKES 10

1 quantity sweet shortcrust
   pastry (see page 304)
2 medium eggs
50 g/2 oz caster sugar
250 ml/9 fl oz golden syrup

40 g/1½ oz butter, melted
50 ml/2 fl oz whipping cream
1 tsp vanilla or
   almond essence
225 g/8 oz unsalted

macadamia nuts,
   coarsely chopped
150 g/5 oz white chocolate,
   coarsely chopped

Preheat the oven to 200°C/400°F/Gas Mark 6, 15 minutes before baking. Roll the pastry out on a lightly floured surface and use to line ten 7.5–9 cm/3–3½ inch tartlet tins. Line each tin with a small piece of tinfoil and fill with baking beans. Arrange on a baking sheet and bake blind in the preheated oven for 10 minutes. Remove the tinfoil and baking beans and leave to cool.

Beat the eggs with the sugar until light and creamy, then beat in the golden syrup, the butter, cream and vanilla or almond essence. Stir in the macadamia nuts. Sprinkle 100 g/3½ oz of the chopped white chocolate equally over the bases of the tartlet cases and divide the mixture evenly among them.

Reduce the oven temperature to 180°C/350°F/Gas Mark 4 and bake the tartlets for 20 minutes, or until the tops are puffy and golden and the filling is set. Remove from the oven and leave to cool on a wire rack.

Carefully remove the tartlets from their tins and arrange closely together on the wire rack. Melt the remaining white chocolate and, using a teaspoon or a small paper piping bag, drizzle the melted chocolate over the surface of the tartlets in a zig-zag pattern. Serve slightly warm or at room temperature.

Try this: FOR AN ALTERNATIVE: 278 FOR KIDS: 260

Chocolate Peanut Butter Pie

CUTS INTO 8 SLICES

22–24 chocolate wafers or
    peanut butter cookies
100 g/3½ oz butter, melted
1–2 tbsp sugar
1 tsp vanilla essence
1½ tbsp gelatine
100 g/3½ oz caster sugar

1 tbsp cornflour
½ tsp salt
225 ml/8 fl oz milk
2 large eggs, separated
2 large egg yolks
100 g/3½ oz plain dark
    chocolate, chopped

2 tbsp rum or 2 tsp
    vanilla essence
125 g/4 oz smooth
    peanut butter
300 ml/½ pint
    whipping cream
chocolate curls, to decorate

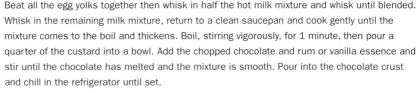

Place the wafers or cookies with the melted butter, sugar and vanilla essence in a food processor and blend together. Press into the base of 23 cm/9 inch pie plate or flat tin. Chill in the refrigerator for 15–20 minutes. Place 3 tablespoons of cold water in a bowl and sprinkle over the powdered gelatine. Leave until softened. Blend half the sugar with the cornflour and salt in a heavy-based saucepan and gradually whisk in the milk. Bring to the boil, then reduce the heat and boil gently for 1–2 minutes, or until thickened and smooth, stirring constantly.

Beat all the egg yolks together then whisk in half the hot milk mixture and whisk until blended. Whisk in the remaining milk mixture, return to a clean saucepan and cook gently until the mixture comes to the boil and thickens. Boil, stirring vigorously, for 1 minute, then pour a quarter of the custard into a bowl. Add the chopped chocolate and rum or vanilla essence and stir until the chocolate has melted and the mixture is smooth. Pour into the chocolate crust and chill in the refrigerator until set.

Whisk the softened gelatine into the remaining custard and whisk until thoroughly dissolved. Whisk in the peanut butter until melted and smooth. Whisk the egg whites until stiff, then whisk in the remaining sugar, 1 tablespoon at a time. Whip the cream until soft peaks form. Fold 125 ml/4 fl oz of the cream into the custard, then fold in the egg whites. Spread the peanut butter cream mixture over the chocolate layer. Spread the surface with the remaining cream, decorate with chocolate curls and chill in the refrigerator until ready to serve.

Try this: FOR AN ALTERNATIVE: 74   FOR KIDS: 228

Chocolate Meringue Nest with Fruity Filling

SERVES 8

125 g/4 oz hazelnuts, toasted
125 g/4 oz golden
   caster sugar
75 g/3 oz plain dark
   chocolate, broken
   into pieces
2 medium egg whites

pinch of salt
1 tsp cornflour
½ tsp white wine vinegar
chocolate curls, to decorate

For the filling:
150 ml/¼ pint double cream

150 g/5 oz mascarpone
   cheese
prepared summer fruits,
   such as strawberries,
   raspberries and
   redcurrants

Preheat the oven to 110°C/225°F/Gas Mark ¼, 5 minutes before baking and line a baking sheet with non-stick baking parchment. Place the hazelnuts and 2 tablespoons of the caster sugar in a food processor and blend to a powder. Add the chocolate and blend again until the chocolate is roughly chopped.

In a clean, grease-free bowl, whisk the egg whites and salt until soft peaks form. Gradually whisk in the remaining sugar a teaspoonful at a time and continue to whisk until the meringue is stiff and shiny. Fold in the cornflour and the white wine vinegar with the chocolate and hazelnut mixture.

Spoon the mixture into eight mounds, about 10 cm/4 inches in diameter, on the baking parchment. Do not worry if they are not perfect shapes. Make a hollow in each mound, then place in the preheated oven. Cook for 1½ hours, then switch the oven off and leave in the oven until cool.

To make the filling, whip the cream until soft peaks form. In another bowl, beat the mascarpone cheese until it is softened, then mix with the cream. Spoon the mixture into the meringue nests and top with the fresh fruits. Decorate with a few chocolate curls and serve.

Try this: FOR AN ALTERNATIVE: 80   FOR KIDS: 222

Mini Pistachio & Chocolate Strudels

MAKES 24

5 large sheets filo pastry
50 g/2 oz butter, melted
1–2 tbsp caster sugar
 for sprinkling
50 g/2 oz white chocolate,

melted, to decorate
For the filling:
125 g/4 oz unsalted
 pistachios, finely chopped
3 tbsp caster sugar

50 g/2 oz plain dark
 chocolate, finely chopped
1–2 tsp rosewater
1 tbsp icing sugar
 for dusting

Preheat the oven to 170°C/325°F/Gas Mark 3, 10 minutes before baking. Lightly oil two large baking sheets. For the filling, mix the finely chopped pistachio nuts, the sugar and dark chocolate in a bowl. Sprinkle with the rosewater and stir lightly together and reserve.

Cut each filo pastry sheet to make 23 x 18 cm/9 x 7 inch rectangles. Place one rectangle on the work surface and brush with a little melted butter. Place another rectangle on top and brush with a little more butter. Sprinkle with a little caster sugar and spread about 1 dessertspoon of the filling along one short end. Fold the short end over the filling, then fold in the long edges and roll up. Place on the baking sheet seam-side down. Continue with the remaining pastry sheets and filling until both are used.

Brush each strudel with the remaining melted butter and sprinkle with a little caster sugar. Bake in the preheated oven for 20 minutes, or until golden brown and the pastry is crisp.

Remove from the oven and leave on the baking sheet for 2 minutes, then transfer to a wire rack. Dust with icing sugar. Place the melted white chocolate in a small piping bag fitted with a plain writing pipe and pipe squiggles over the strudel. Leave to set before serving.

Try this: FOR AN ALTERNATIVE: 276   FOR KIDS: 344

Chocolate Mousse in Filo Cups

SERVES 6

6 large sheets filo pastry,
   thawed if frozen
40 g/1½ oz unsalted
   butter, melted
1 tbsp caster sugar
3 x 60 g/2½ oz Mars bars,
   coarsely chopped

1½ tbsp milk
300 ml/½ pint double cream
1 large egg white
1 tsp cocoa powder
1 tbsp plain dark grated
   chocolate
chocolate sauce (see page

280), to serve (optional)

For the topping:
300 ml/½ pint whipping cream
125 g/4 oz white
   chocolate, grated
1 tsp vanilla essence

Preheat the oven to 180°C/350°F/Gas Mark 4, 10 minutes before baking. Lightly oil six 150 ml/¼ pint ramekins. Cut the filo pastry into 15 cm/6 inch squares, place one square on the work surface, then brush with a little of the melted butter and sprinkle with a little caster sugar. Butter a second square and lay it over the first at an angle, sprinkle with a little more caster sugar and repeat with two more pastry squares. Press the assembled filo pastry into the oiled ramekin, pressing into the base to make a flat bottom and keeping the edges pointing up. Continue making the cups in this way, then place on a baking sheet and bake in the preheated oven for 10–15 minutes or until crisp and golden. Remove and leave to cool before removing the filo cups from the ramekins. Leave until cold.

Melt the Mars bars and milk in a small saucepan, stirring constantly until melted and smooth. Leave to cool for 10 minutes, stirring occasionally. Whisk the cream until thick and stir a spoonful into the melted chocolate mixture, then fold in the remaining cream. Whisk the egg white until stiff and fold into the chocolate mixture together with the cocoa powder. Chill the mousse in the refrigerator for 2–3 hours. For the topping, boil 125 ml/4 fl oz of the whipping cream, add the grated white chocolate and vanilla essence and stir until smooth, then strain into a bowl and leave to cool. Whisk the remaining cream until thick, then fold into the white chocolate cream mixture. Spoon the mousse into the filo cups, cover with the cream mixture and sprinkle with grated chocolate. Chill before serving with chocolate sauce, if liked.

Try this: FOR AN ALTERNATIVE: 282   FOR KIDS: 284

Raspberry Chocolate Ganache & Berry Tartlets

SERVES 8

1 quantity chocolate pastry
  (see page 302)
600 ml/1 pint whipping cream
275 g/10 oz seedless

raspberry jam
225 g/8 oz plain dark
  chocolate, chopped
700 g/1½ lb raspberries or

other summer berries
50 ml/2 fl oz framboise liqueur
1 tbsp caster sugar
crème fraîche, to serve

Preheat the oven to 200°C/400°F/Gas Mark 6, 15 minutes before cooking. Make the chocolate pastry and use to line eight 7.5 cm/3 inch tartlet tins. Bake blind in the preheated oven for 12 minutes.

Place 400 ml/14 fl oz of the cream and half of the raspberry jam in a saucepan and bring to the boil, whisking constantly to dissolve the jam. Remove from the heat and add the chocolate all at once, stirring until the chocolate has melted.

Pour into the pastry-lined tartlet tins, shaking gently to distribute the ganache evenly. Chill in the refrigerator for 1 hour or until set.

Place the berries in a large shallow bowl. Heat the remaining raspberry jam with half the framboise liqueur over a medium heat until melted and bubbling. Drizzle over the berries and toss gently to coat. Divide the berries among the tartlets, piling them up if necessary. Chill in the refrigerator until ready to serve.

Remove the tartlets from the refrigerator for at least 30 minutes before serving. Using an electric whisk, whisk the remaining cream with the caster sugar and the remaining framboise liqueur until it is thick and softly peaking. Serve with the tartlets and crème fraîche.

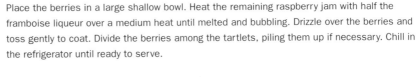

Try this: FOR AN ALTERNATIVE: 300 FOR KIDS: 296

Chocolaty Puffs

MAKES 12 LARGE PUFFS

For the choux pastry:
150 g/5 oz plain flour
2 tbsp cocoa powder
½ tsp salt
1 tbsp sugar
125 g/4 oz butter,
   cut into pieces
5 large eggs

For the chocolate
   cream filling:
225 g/8 oz plain dark
   chocolate, chopped
600 ml/1 pint double cream
1 tbsp caster sugar (optional)
2 tbsp crème de cacao
   (optional)

For the chocolate sauce:
225 g/8 oz plain dark chocolate
300 ml/½ pint whipping
   cream
50 g/2 oz butter, diced
1–2 tbsp golden syrup
1 tsp vanilla essence

Preheat the oven to 220°C/425°F/Gas Mark 7, 15 minutes before baking. Lightly oil a large baking sheet. To make the choux pastry, sift the flour and cocoa powder together. Place 250 ml/9 fl oz of water, the salt, sugar and butter in a saucepan and bring to the boil. Remove from the heat and add the flour mixture all at once, beating vigorously with a wooden spoon until the mixture forms a ball in the centre of the saucepan. Return to the heat and cook for 1 minute stirring, then cool slightly. Using an electric mixer, beat in four of the eggs, one at a time, beating well after each addition. Beat the last egg and add a little at a time until the dough is thick and shiny. Pipe or spoon 12 large puffs onto the prepared baking sheet, leaving space between them. Cook in the preheated oven for 30–35 minutes, or until puffy and golden. Remove from the oven, slice off the top third of each bun and return to the oven for 5 minutes to dry out. Remove and leave to cool.

For the filling, heat the chocolate with 125 ml/4 fl oz of the double cream and 1 tablespoon of caster sugar, if using, stirring until smooth, then leave to cool. Whisk the remaining cream until soft peaks form and stir in the crème de cacao, if using. Quickly fold the cream into the chocolate, then spoon or pipe into the choux buns and place the lids on top. Place all the ingredients for the sauce in a small saucepan and heat gently, stirring until smooth. Remove from the heat and leave to cool, stirring occasionally. Pour over the puffs and serve.

Try this: FOR AN ALTERNATIVE: 288 FOR KIDS: 222

White Chocolate Mousse & Strawberry Tart

CUTS INTO 10 SLICES

1 quantity sweet shortcrust
    pastry (see page 304)
60 g/2½ oz strawberry jam
1–2 tbsp kirsch or
    framboise liqueur
450–700 g/1–1½ lb ripe

strawberries, sliced
    lengthways

For the white
    chocolate mousse:
250 g/9 oz white

chocolate, chopped
350 ml/12 oz double cream
3 tbsp kirsch or framboise
    liqueur
1–2 large egg whites (optional)

Preheat the oven to 200°C/400°F/Gas Mark 6, 15 minutes before baking. Roll the prepared pastry out on a lightly floured surface and use to line a 25.5 cm/10 inch flan tin. Line with either tinfoil or non-stick baking parchment and baking beans then bake blind in the preheated oven for 15–20 minutes. Remove the tinfoil or baking parchment and return to the oven for a further 5 minutes.

To make the mousse, place the white chocolate with 2 tablespoons of water and 125 ml/4 fl oz of the cream in a saucepan and heat gently, stirring until the chocolate has melted and is smooth. Remove from the heat, stir in the kirsch or framboise liqueur and cool. Whip the remaining cream until soft peaks form. Fold a spoonful of the cream into the cooled white chocolate mixture, then fold in the remaining cream. If using, whisk the egg whites until stiff and gently fold into the white chocolate cream mixture to make a softer, lighter mousse. Chill in the refrigerator for 15–20 minutes.

Heat the strawberry jam with the kirsch or framboise liqueur and brush or spread half the mixture onto the pastry base. Leave to cool. Spread the chilled chocolate mousse over the jam and arrange the sliced strawberries in concentric circles over the mousse. If necessary, reheat the strawberry jam and glaze the strawberries lightly. Chill the tart in the refrigerator for about 3–4 hours, or until the chocolate mousse has set. Cut into slices and serve.

Try this: FOR AN ALTERNATIVE: 302   FOR KIDS: 128

Chocolate Creams

SERVES 4

125 g/4 oz plain dark
   chocolate
1 tbsp brandy
4 medium eggs, separated

200 ml/7 fl oz pint
   double cream
1 tbsp caster sugar
grated rind of 1 orange

2 tbsp Cointreau
25 g/1 oz white chocolate
8 physalis, to decorate

Break the chocolate into small pieces, then place in a heatproof bowl set over a saucepan of gently simmering water. Add the brandy and heat gently, stirring occasionally until the chocolate has melted and is smooth. Remove from the heat and leave to cool slightly, then beat in the egg yolks, one at a time, beating well after each addition. Reserve.

Whisk the egg whites until stiff but not dry, then stir 1 tablespoon into the chocolate mixture. Add the remainder and stir in gently. Chill in the refrigerator while preparing the cream.

Whip the cream until just beginning to thicken, then stir in the sugar, orange rind and Cointreau and continue to whisk together until soft peaks form. Spoon the chocolate mousse into the cream mixture and using a metal spoon, fold the two mixtures together to create a marbled effect. Spoon into four individual glass dishes, cover each dessert with clingfilm and chill in the refrigerator for 2 hours.

Using a vegetable peeler, shave the white chocolate into curls. Uncover the desserts and scatter over the shavings. Peel the husks back from the physalis berries and pinch together for decoration. Top each dessert with two berries and chill in the refrigerator until ready to serve.

Try this: FOR AN ALTERNATIVE: 318   FOR KIDS: 332

Brandied Raisin Chocolate Mousse

SERVES 4

125 g/4 oz raisins
1 tsp soft brown sugar
3 tbsp brandy
200 g/7 oz plain dark chocolate

150 ml/¼ pint ready-made
   custard
300 ml/½ pint double cream
1 tbsp strong black coffee

1 medium egg white
50 ml/2 fl oz freshly
   whipped cream
chocolate curls, to decorate

Place the raisins in a bowl together with the sugar, then pour over the brandy. Stir well and cover with clingfilm. Leave to marinate overnight or until the raisins have absorbed most, or all of the brandy. Stir occasionally during marinating.

Break the chocolate into small pieces and place in a small heatproof bowl set over a saucepan of gently simmering water. Heat gently, stirring occasionally, until the chocolate has melted and is smooth. Remove the bowl from the heat and leave to stand for about 10 minutes, or until the chocolate cools and begins to thicken. Using a metal spoon or rubber spatula, carefully fold in the prepared custard.

Whip the cream until soft peaks form and fold into the chocolate custard mixture together with the coffee. Gently stir in the brandy-soaked raisins with any remaining brandy left in the bowl.

Whisk the egg white in a clean, grease-free bowl, until stiff but not dry, then fold 1 tablespoon into the chocolate mixture and mix together lightly. Add the remaining egg white and stir lightly until well mixed. Spoon into four tall glasses and chill in the refrigerator for up to 2 hours.

Just before serving, pipe a swirl of whipped cream on the top of each mousse and decorate with the chocolate curls, then serve.

Try this: FOR AN ALTERNATIVE: 258   FOR KIDS: 344

Chocolate Profiteroles

SERVES 4

For the pastry:
150 ml/¼ pint water
50 g/2 oz butter
65 g/2½ oz plain flour, sifted
2 medium eggs,
    lightly beaten

For the custard:
300 ml/½ pint milk
pinch of freshly
    grated nutmeg
3 medium egg yolks
50 g/2 oz caster sugar
2 tbsp plain flour, sifted
2 tbsp cornflour, sifted

For the sauce:
175 g/6 oz soft brown sugar
150 ml/¼ pint boiling water
1 tsp instant coffee
1 tbsp cocoa powder
1 tbsp brandy
75 g/3 oz butter
1 tbsp golden syrup

Preheat the oven to 220°C/425°F/Gas Mark 7, 15 minutes before cooking. Lightly oil two baking sheets. For the pastry, place the water and the butter in a heavy-based saucepan and bring to the boil. Remove from the heat and beat in the flour. Return to the heat and cook for 1 minute or until the mixture forms a ball in the centre of the saucepan.

Remove from the heat and leave to cool slightly, then gradually beat in the eggs a little at a time, beating well after each addition. Once all the eggs have been added, beat until the paste is smooth and glossy. Pipe or spoon 20 small balls onto the baking sheets, allowing plenty of room for expansion. Bake in the preheated oven for 25 minutes or until well risen and golden. Reduce the oven temperature to 180°C/350°F/Gas Mark 4. Make a hole in each ball and continue to bake for a further 5 minutes. Remove from the oven and leave to cool.

For the custard, place the milk and nutmeg in a heavy-based saucepan and bring to the boil. In another saucepan, whisk together the egg yolks, sugar and the flours, then beat in the hot milk. Bring to the boil and simmer, whisking constantly for 2 minutes. Cover and leave to cool. Spoon the custard into the profiteroles and arrange on a large serving dish. Place all the sauce ingredients in a small saucepan and bring to the boil, then simmer for 10 minutes. Remove from the heat and cool slightly before serving with the chocolate profiteroles.

Try this: FOR AN ALTERNATIVE: 280   FOR KIDS: 218

Chocolate Rice Pudding

SERVES 4

60 g/2½ oz pudding rice
75 g/3 oz caster sugar
1 x 410 g can evaporated
  milk
600 ml/1 pint milk

pinch of freshly
  grated nutmeg
¼ tsp ground cinnamon,
  optional
50 g/2 oz plain chocolate

chips
25 g/1 oz butter
freshly sliced strawberries,
  to decorate
crème fraîche, to serve

Preheat the oven to 170°C/325°F/Gas Mark 3, 10 minutes before cooking. Lightly butter a large ovenproof dish. Rinse the pudding rice, then place in the base of the buttered dish and sprinkle over the caster sugar.

Pour the evaporated milk and milk into a heavy-based saucepan and bring slowly to the boil over a low heat, stirring occasionally to avoid sticking. Pour the milk over the rice and sugar and stir well until well mixed and the sugar has dissolved.

Grate a little nutmeg over the top, then sprinkle with the ground cinnamon, if liked. Cover tightly with tinfoil and bake in the preheated oven for 30 minutes.

Remove the pudding from the oven and stir well to break up any lumps that may have formed. Cover with tinfoil and return to the oven for a further 30 minutes. Remove the pudding from the oven once again and stir to break up any more lumps.

Stir the chocolate chips into the rice pudding and then dot with the butter. Continue to bake, uncovered, in the oven for a further 45 minutes–1 hour, or until the rice is tender and the skin is golden brown. Serve warm, with or without the skin, according to personal preference. Serve with a few sliced strawberries and a spoonful of crème fraîche.

Try this: FOR AN ALTERNATIVE: 306   FOR KIDS: 300

Hazelnut Meringues with Chocolate Sauce

SERVES 6

4 medium egg whites
225 g/8 oz caster sugar
125 g/4 oz ground hazelnuts
50 g/2 oz toasted hazelnuts,
    sliced
fresh berries, such as

raspberries, strawberries
    and blueberries,
    to serve

For the chocolate sauce:
225 g/8 oz plain dark

chocolate, broken
    into pieces
50 g/2 oz butter
300 ml/½ pint double cream
1 tbsp golden syrup

Preheat the oven to 150°C/300°F/Gas Mark 2, 10 minutes before baking. Line two baking sheets with non-stick baking parchment. Whisk the egg whites in a large grease-free bowl until stiff, then add the caster sugar, 1 teaspoonful at a time, whisking well after each addition. Continue to whisk until the mixture is stiff and dry, then using a metal spoon, fold in the ground hazelnuts.

Using 2 dessertspoons, spoon the mixture into 12 quenelle shapes onto the baking parchment. Sprinkle over the ground hazelnuts and bake in the preheated oven for 1½–2 hours or until dry and crisp. Switch the oven off and leave to cool in the oven.

To make the chocolate sauce, place the chocolate with the butter and 4 tablespoons of the cream and the golden syrup in a heavy-based saucepan and heat, stirring occasionally, until the chocolate has melted and the mixture is blended. Do not boil. Whip the remaining cream until soft peaks form.

Sandwich the meringues together with the whipped cream and place on serving plates. Spoon over the sauce and serve with a fresh berries.

Try this: FOR AN ALTERNATIVE: 272   FOR KIDS: 80

Frozen Mississippi Mud Pie

CUTS 6-8 SLICES

1 quantity ginger crumb
crust (see page 240)
600 ml/1 pint chocolate
ice cream
600 ml/1 pint coffee-

flavoured ice cream

For the chocolate topping:
175 g/6 oz plain dark
chocolate, chopped

50 ml/2 fl oz single cream
1 tbsp golden syrup
1 tsp vanilla essence
50 g/2 oz coarsely grated
white and milk chocolate

Prepare the crumb crust and use to line a 23 cm/9 inch loose-based flan tin and freeze for 30 minutes.

Soften the ice creams at room temperature for about 25 minutes. Spoon the chocolate ice cream into the crumb crust, spreading it evenly over the base, then spoon the coffee ice cream over the chocolate ice cream, mounding it slightly in the centre. Return to the freezer to refreeze the ice cream.

For the topping, heat the dark chocolate with the cream, golden syrup and vanilla essence in a saucepan. Stir until the chocolate has melted and is smooth. Pour into a bowl and chill in the refrigerator, stirring occasionally, until cold but not set.

Spread the cooled chocolate mixture over the top of the frozen pie. Sprinkle with the chocolate and return to the freezer for 1½ hours or until firm. Serve at room temperature.

Try this: FOR AN ALTERNATIVE: 124   FOR KIDS: 120

Chocolate Lemon Tartlets

MAKES 10

1 quantity chocolate pastry
  (see page 302)
175 ml/6 fl oz double cream
175 g/6 oz plain dark
  chocolate, chopped

2 tbsp butter, diced
1 tsp vanilla essence
350 g/12 oz lemon curd
225 ml/8 fl oz prepared
  custard sauce

225 ml/8 fl oz single cream
½ –1 tsp almond essence

To decorate: grated chocolate
toasted flaked almonds

Preheat the oven to 200°C/400°F/Gas Mark 6, 15 minutes before baking. Roll the prepared pastry out on a lightly floured surface and use to line ten 7.5 cm/3 inch tartlet tins. Place a small piece of crumpled tinfoil in each and bake blind in the preheated oven for 12 minutes. Remove from the oven and leave to cool.

Bring the cream to the boil, then remove from the heat and add the chocolate all at once. Stir until smooth and melted. Beat in the butter and vanilla essence and pour into the tartlets and leave to cool.

Beat the lemon curd until soft and spoon a thick layer over the chocolate in each tartlet, spreading gently to the edges. Do not chill in the refrigerator or the chocolate will be too firm.

Place the prepared custard sauce into a large bowl and gradually whisk in the cream and almond essence until the custard is smooth and runny.

To serve, spoon a little custard onto a plate and place a tartlet in the centre. Sprinkle with grated chocolate and almonds, then serve.

Try this: FOR AN ALTERNATIVE: 278 FOR KIDS: 108

Chocolate Fruit Pizza

SERVES 8

1 quantity chocolate pastry
   (see page 302)
2 tbsp chocolate spread
1 small peach, very thinly sliced
1 small nectarine, very
   thinly sliced
150 g/5 oz strawberries,

halved or quartered
75 g/3 oz raspberries
75 g/3 oz blueberries
75 g/3 oz plain dark
   chocolate, coarsely
   chopped
1 tbsp butter, melted

2 tbsp sugar
75 g/3 oz white
   chocolate, chopped
1 tbsp hazelnuts, toasted
   and chopped
sprigs of fresh mint, to
   decorate

Preheat the oven to 200°C/400°F/Gas Mark 6, 15 minutes before baking. Lightly oil a large baking sheet. Roll the prepared pastry out to a 23 cm/9 inch round and place the pastry round onto the baking sheet, and crimp the edges. Using a fork, prick the base all over and chill in the refrigerator for 30 minutes.

Line the pastry with tinfoil and weigh down with an ovenproof flat dinner plate or base of a large flan tin and bake blind in the preheated oven until the edges begin to colour. Remove from the oven and discard the weight and tinfoil.

Carefully spread the chocolate spread over the pizza base and arrange the peach and nectarine slices around the outside edge in overlapping circles. Toss the berries with the plain chocolate and arrange in the centre. Drizzle with the melted butter and sprinkle with the sugar. Bake in the preheated oven for 10–12 minutes, or until the fruit begins to soften. Transfer the pizza to a wire rack.

Sprinkle the white chocolate and hazelnuts over the surface and return to the oven for 1 minute or until the chocolate begins to soften. If the pastry starts to darken too much, cover the edge with strips of tinfoil. Remove to a wire rack and leave to cool. Decorate with sprigs of fresh mint and serve warm.

Try this: FOR AN ALTERNATIVE: 302   FOR KIDS: 116

Rice Pudding & Chocolate Tart

SERVES 8

1 quantity chocolate pastry
   (see page 302)
1 tsp cocoa powder for dusting

For the chocolate ganache:
200 ml/7 fl oz double cream
1 tbsp golden syrup
175 g/6 oz plain dark

chocolate, chopped
1 tbsp butter
1 tsp vanilla essence

For the rice pudding:
1 litre/1¾ pints milk
½ tsp salt
1 vanilla pod

100 g/3½ oz long-grain
   white rice
1 tbsp cornflour
2 tbsp sugar

To decorate:
few fresh blueberries
sprigs of fresh mint

Preheat the oven to 200°C/400°F/Gas Mark 6, 15 minutes before baking. Roll the chocolate pastry out and use to line a 23 cm/9 inch flan tin. Place a sheet of non-stick baking parchment and baking beans in the tin and bake blind in the preheated oven for 15 minutes.

For the ganache, place the cream and golden syrup in a heavy-based saucepan and bring to the boil. Remove from the heat and add the chocolate all at once, stirring until smooth. Beat in the butter and vanilla essence, pour into the baked pastry case and reserve.

For the rice pudding, bring the milk and salt to the boil in a medium-sized saucepan. Split the vanilla pod and scrape the seeds into the milk and add the vanilla pod. Sprinkle in the rice, then bring to the boil. Reduce the heat and simmer until the rice is tender and the milk is creamy. Remove from the heat.

Blend the cornflour and sugar together, then stir in 2 tablespoons of water to make a paste. Stir a little of the hot rice mixture into the cornflour mixture, then stir the cornflour mixture into the rice. Bring to the boil and cook, stirring constantly until thickened. Set the base of the saucepan into a bowl of iced water and stir until cooled and thickened. Spoon the rice pudding into the tart, smoothing the surface. Leave to set. Dust with cocoa powder, and decorate with a few blueberries and some fresh mint to serve.

Try this: FOR AN ALTERNATIVE: 128   FOR KIDS: 228

Pear & Chocolate Custard Tart

CUTS INTO 6-8 SLICES

For the chocolate pastry:
125 g/4 oz unsalted butter, softened
60 g/2½ oz caster sugar
2 tsp vanilla essence
175 g/6 oz plain flour, sifted

40 g/1½ oz cocoa powder

For the filling:
125 g/4 oz plain dark chocolate, chopped
225 ml/8 fl oz whipping cream

50 g/2 oz caster sugar
1 large egg
1 large egg yolk
1 tbsp crème de cacao
3 ripe pears

Preheat the oven to 190°C/375°F/Gas Mark 5, 10 minutes before baking. To make the pastry, put the butter, sugar and vanilla essence into a food processor and blend until creamy. Add the flour and cocoa powder and process until a soft dough forms. Remove the dough, wrap in clingfilm and chill in the refrigerator for at least 1 hour. Roll out the dough between two sheets of clingfilm to a 28 cm/11 inch round. Peel off the top sheet of clingfilm and invert the pastry round into a lightly oiled 23 cm/9 inch loose-based flan tin, easing the dough into the base and sides. Prick the base with a fork, then chill in the refrigerator for 1 hour. Place a sheet of non-stick baking parchment and baking beans in the case and bake blind in the preheated oven for 10 minutes. Remove the parchment and beans and bake for a further 5 minutes. Remove and cool.

To make the filling, heat the chocolate, cream and half the sugar in a medium saucepan over a low heat, stirring until melted and smooth. Remove from the heat and cool slightly before beating in the egg, egg yolk and crème de cacao. Spread evenly over the pastry case base. Peel the pears, then cut each pear in half and carefully remove the core. Cut each half crossways into thin slices and arrange over the custard, gently fanning the slices towards the centre and pressing into the chocolate custard. Bake in the oven for 10 minutes. Reduce the oven temperature to 180°C/350°F/Gas Mark 4 and sprinkle the surface evenly with the remaining sugar. Bake in the oven for 20–25 minutes, or until the custard is set and the pears are tender. Remove from the oven and leave to cool slightly. Cut into slices and serve.

Try this: FOR AN ALTERNATIVE: 224 FOR KIDS: 126

Chocolate, Orange & Pine Nut Tart

CUTS INTO 8-10 SLICES

For the sweet
shortcrust pastry:
150 g/5 oz plain flour
½ tsp salt
3–4 tbsp icing sugar
125 g/4 oz unsalted
butter, diced

2 medium egg yolks, beaten
½ tsp vanilla essence

For the filling:
125 g/4 oz plain dark
chocolate, chopped
60 g/2½ oz pine nuts, lightly

toasted
2 large eggs
grated zest of 1 orange
1 tbsp Cointreau
225 ml/8 fl oz whipping
cream
2 tbsp orange marmalade

Preheat the oven to 200°C/400°F/Gas Mark 6, 15 minutes before baking. Place the flour, salt and sugar in a food processor with the butter and blend briefly. Add the egg yolks, 2 tablespoons of iced water and the vanilla essence and blend until a soft dough is formed. Remove and knead until smooth, wrap in clingfilm and chill in the refrigerator for 1 hour.

Lightly oil a 23 cm/9 inch loose-based flan tin. Roll the dough out on a lightly floured surface to a 28 cm/11 inch round and use to line the tin. Press into the sides of the flan tin, crimp the edges, prick the base with a fork and chill in the refrigerator for 1 hour. Bake blind in the preheated oven for 10 minutes. Remove and place on a baking sheet. Reduce the oven temperature to 190°C/375°F/Gas Mark 5.

To make the filling, sprinkle the chocolate and the pine nuts evenly over the base of the pastry case. Beat the eggs, orange zest, Cointreau and cream in a bowl until well blended, then pour over the chocolate and pine nuts.

Bake in the oven for 30 minutes, or until the pastry is golden and the custard mixture is just set. Transfer to a wire rack to cool slightly. Heat the marmalade with 1 tablespoon of water and brush over the tart. Serve warm or at room temperature.

Try this: FOR AN ALTERNATIVE: 118 FOR KIDS: 232

Chocolate Rice Pudding Brûlée

SERVES 6

2 tbsp cocoa powder
75 g/3 oz short-grain rice
600 ml/1 pint milk
1 bay leaf

grated zest of 1 orange
50 g/2 oz white chocolate,
  roughly chopped
1 tbsp golden caster sugar

4 medium egg yolks
225 ml/8 fl oz double cream
½ tsp vanilla essence
4 tbsp demerara sugar

Preheat the oven to 150°C/300°F/Gas Mark 2, 10 minutes before cooking. Preheat the grill on high when ready to use. Gradually blend the cocoa powder with 3 tablespoons of boiling water to form a soft, smooth paste. Place the rice and milk, bay leaf, orange zest and the cocoa powder paste in a saucepan. Bring to the boil, stirring constantly.

Reduce the heat and simmer for 20 minutes, or until the rice is tender. Remove from the heat and discard the bay leaf, then add the white chocolate and stir until melted.

Whisk together the caster sugar and egg yolks until thick, then stir in the cream. Stir in the rice mixture together with the vanilla essence. Pour into a buttered shallow dish. Stand the dish in a baking tin with sufficient hot water to come halfway up the sides of the dish.

Cook in the preheated oven for 1½ hours or until set. Stir occasionally during cooking, either removing the skin from the top or stirring the skin into the pudding. Remove from the tin and leave until cool.

When ready to serve, sprinkle the demerara sugar over the surface of the rice pudding. Place under the preheated grill and cook until the sugar melts and caramelises, turning the dish occasionally. Either serve immediately or chill in the refrigerator for 1 hour before serving.

Try this: FOR AN ALTERNATIVE: 130   FOR KIDS: 246

White Chocolate Cheesecake

CUTS INTO 16 SLICES

For the base:
150 g/5 oz digestive biscuits
50 g/2 oz whole almonds,
    lightly toasted
50 g/2 oz butter, melted
½ tsp almond essence

For the filling:
350 g/12 oz good-quality
    white chocolate, chopped
125 ml/4 fl oz double cream
700 g/1½ lb cream
    cheese, softened
50 g/2 oz caster sugar
4 large eggs

2 tbsp Amaretto or
    almond-flavour liqueur
For the topping:
450 ml/¾ pint soured cream
50 g/2 oz caster sugar
⅛ tsp almond or vanilla essence
white chocolate curls,
    to decorate

Preheat the oven to 180˚C/350˚F/Gas Mark 4, 10 minutes before baking. Lightly oil a 23 x 7.5 cm/9 x 3 inch springform tin. Crush the biscuits and almonds in a food processor to form fine crumbs. Pour in the butter and almond essence and blend. Pour the crumbs into the tin and using the back of a spoon, press on to the bottom and up the sides to within 1 cm/½ inch of the top of the tin. Bake in the preheated oven for 5 minutes to set. Remove and transfer to a wire rack. Reduce the oven temperature to 150˚C/300˚F/Gas Mark 2.

Heat the white chocolate and cream in a saucepan over a low heat, stirring until melted, then cool. Beat the cream cheese and sugar until smooth. Add the eggs, one at a time, beating well after each. Slowly beat in the cooled white chocolate cream and the Amaretto and pour into the baked crust. Place on a baking tray and bake for 45–55 minutes, until the edge of the cake is firm, but the centre is slightly soft. Reduce the oven temperature if the top begins to brown. Remove to a wire rack and increase the temperature to 200˚C/400˚F/Gas Mark 6.

To make the topping, beat the soured cream, sugar and almond or vanilla essence until smooth and pour evenly over the cheesecake. Bake for another 5 minutes to set. Turn off the oven and leave the door halfway open for about 1 hour. Transfer to a wire rack and run a sharp knife around the edge to separate from the tin. Refrigerate until chilled. Remove from the tin, decorate with white chocolate curls and serve.

Steamed Chocolate Chip Pudding

SERVES 6

175 g/6 oz self-raising flour
½ tsp baking powder
75 g/3 oz fresh white
   breadcrumbs
125 g/4 oz shredded suet
125 g/4 oz golden
   caster sugar

2 medium eggs,
   lightly beaten
1 tsp vanilla essence
125 g/4 oz chocolate chips
150 ml/¼ pint cold milk
grated chocolate,
   to decorate

For the chocolate custard:
300 ml/½ pint milk
1 tbsp cornflour
1 tbsp cocoa powder
1 tbsp caster sugar
½ tsp vanilla essence
1 medium egg yolk

Lightly oil a 1.1 litre/2 pint pudding basin and line the base with a small circle of non-stick baking parchment. Sift the flour and baking powder into a bowl, add the breadcrumbs, suet and sugar and mix well. Stir in the eggs and vanilla essence with the chocolate chips and mix with sufficient cold milk to form a smooth dropping consistency.

Spoon the mixture into the prepared basin and cover the pudding with a double sheet of baking parchment and then either a double sheet of tinfoil or a pudding cloth, with a pleat in the centre to allow for expansion. Secure tightly with string.

Place in the top of a steamer, set over a saucepan of simmering water and steam for 1½–2 hours, or until the pudding is cooked and firm to the touch – replenish the water as necessary. Remove and leave to rest for 5 minutes before turning out onto a warmed serving plate.

Meanwhile, make the custard. Blend a little of the milk with the cornflour and cocoa powder to form a paste. Stir in the remaining milk with the sugar and vanilla essence. Pour into a saucepan and bring to the boil, stirring. Whisk in the egg yolk and cook for 1 minute. Decorate the pudding with grated chocolate and serve with the sauce.

Try this: FOR AN ALTERNATIVE: 316 FOR KIDS: 216

Spicy White Chocolate Mousse

SERVES 4-6

6 cardamom pods
125 ml/4 fl oz milk
3 bay leaves

200 g/7 oz white chocolate
300 ml/½ pint double cream
3 medium egg whites

1–2 tsp cocoa powder, sifted,
for dusting

Tap the cardamom pods lightly so they split. Remove the seeds, then, using a pestle and mortar, crush lightly. Pour the milk into a small saucepan and add the crushed seeds and the bay leaves. Bring to the boil gently over a medium heat. Remove from the heat, cover and leave in a warm place for at least 30 minutes to infuse.

Break the chocolate into small pieces and place in a heatproof bowl set over a saucepan of gently simmering water. Ensure the water is not touching the base of the bowl. When the chocolate has melted, remove the bowl from the heat and stir until smooth.

Whip the cream until it has slightly thickened and holds its shape, but does not form peaks. Reserve. Whisk the egg whites in a clean, grease-free bowl until stiff and standing in soft peaks.

Strain the milk through a sieve into the cooled, melted chocolate and beat until smooth. Spoon the chocolate mixture into the egg whites, then using a large metal spoon, fold gently. Add the whipped cream and fold in gently.

Spoon into a large serving dish or individual small cups. Chill in the refrigerator for 3–4 hours. Just before serving, dust with a little sifted cocoa powder and then serve.

Try this: FOR AN ALTERNATIVE: 256   FOR KIDS: 206

Peach & Chocolate Bake

SERVES 6

200 g/7 oz plain dark
   chocolate
125 g/4 oz unsalted butter
4 medium eggs, separated

125 g/4 oz caster sugar
425 g can peach slices,
   drained
½ tsp ground cinnamon

1 tbsp icing sugar, sifted,
   to decorate
crème fraîche, to serve

Preheat the oven to 170°C/325°F/Gas Mark 3, 10 minutes before baking. Lightly oil a
1.7 litre/3 pint ovenproof dish.

Break the chocolate and butter into small pieces and place in a small heatproof bowl set over
a saucepan of gently simmering water. Ensure the water is not touching the base of the bowl
and leave to melt. Remove the bowl from the heat and stir until smooth.

Whisk the egg yolks with the sugar until very thick and creamy, then stir the melted chocolate
and butter into the whisked egg yolk mixture and mix together lightly.

Place the egg whites in a clean, grease-free bowl and whisk until stiff, then fold 2 tablespoons
of the whisked egg whites into the chocolate mixture. Mix well, then add the remaining egg
white and fold in very lightly.

Fold the peach slices and the cinnamon into the mixture, then spoon the mixture into the
prepared dish. Do not level the mixture – leave the surface a little uneven.

Bake in the preheated oven for 35–40 minutes, or until well risen and just firm to the touch.
Sprinkle the bake with the icing sugar and serve immediately with spoonfuls of crème fraîche.

Try this: FOR AN ALTERNATIVE: 100   FOR KIDS: 94

Nutty Date Pudding with Chocolate Sauce

SERVES 6-8

125 g/4 oz butter, softened
125 g/4 oz golden caster sugar
3 medium eggs, beaten
175 g/6 oz self-raising flour, sifted
50 g/2 oz plain dark chocolate, grated

3 tbsp milk
75 g/3 oz hazelnuts, roughly chopped
75 g/3 oz stoned dates, roughly chopped
chopped toasted hazelnuts, to serve

For the chocolate sauce:
50 g/2 oz unsalted butter
50 g/2 oz soft light brown sugar
50 g/2 oz plain dark chocolate, broken into pieces
125 ml/4 fl oz double cream

Lightly oil a 1.1 litre/2 pint pudding basin and line the base with a small circle of non-stick baking parchment. Cream the butter and sugar together in a large bowl until light and fluffy. Add the beaten eggs a little at a time, adding 1 tablespoon of the flour after each addition. When all the eggs have been added, stir in the remaining flour. Add the grated chocolate and mix in lightly, then stir in the milk together with the hazelnuts and dates. Stir lightly until mixed well. Spoon the mixture into the pudding basin and level the surface. Cover with a double sheet of baking parchment with a pleat in the centre, allowing for expansion, then cover either with a pudding cloth or a double sheet of tinfoil, again with a central pleat. Secure with string.

Place in the top of a steamer, set over a saucepan of gently simmering water and steam for 2 hours, or until cooked and firm to the touch. Remember to top up the water if necessary. Remove the pudding from the saucepan and leave to rest for 5 minutes, before turning out onto a serving plate. Discard the small circle of baking parchment, then sprinkle with the chopped toasted hazelnuts. Keep warm.

Meanwhile, make the sauce. Place the butter, sugar and chocolate in a saucepan and heat until the chocolate has melted. Stir in the cream and simmer for 3 minutes until thickened. Pour over the pudding and serve.

Try this: FOR AN ALTERNATIVE: 110   FOR KIDS: 114

Rich Chocolate & Orange Mousse Dessert

SERVES 8

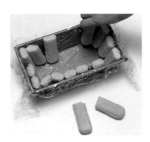

8–12 sponge finger biscuits
225 g/8 oz plain dark
   chocolate, broken
   into pieces
225 g/8 oz unsalted butter

2 tbsp orange flower water
40 g/1½ oz cocoa
   powder, sifted
125 g/4 oz icing sugar, sifted
5 medium eggs, separated

50 g/2 oz caster sugar
1 orange, thinly sliced
300 ml/½ pint double cream

Oil and line a 900 g/2 lb loaf tin with clingfilm, taking care to keep the clingfilm as wrinkle free as possible. Arrange the sponge finger biscuits around the edge of the loaf tin, trimming the biscuits to fit if necessary.

Place the chocolate, butter and orange flower water in a heavy-based saucepan and heat gently, stirring occasionally, until the chocolate has melted and is smooth. Remove the saucepan from the heat, add the cocoa powder and 50 g/2 oz of the icing sugar. Stir until smooth, then beat in the egg yolks. In a clean, grease-free bowl whisk the egg whites until stiff but not dry. Sift in the remaining icing sugar and whisk until stiff and glossy. Fold the egg white mixture into the chocolate mixture and, using a metal spoon or rubber spatula, stir until well blended. Spoon the mousse mixture into the prepared loaf tin and level the surface. Cover and chill in the refrigerator until set.

Meanwhile, place the caster sugar with 150 ml/¼ pint of water in a heavy-based saucepan and heat until the sugar has dissolved. Bring to the boil and boil for 5 minutes. Add the orange slices and simmer for about 2–4 minutes or until the slices become opaque. Drain on absorbent kitchen paper and reserve. Trim the top of the biscuits to the same level as the mousse. Invert onto a plate and remove the tin and clingfilm. Whip the cream until soft peaks form and spoon into a piping bag fitted with a star-shaped nozzle. Pipe swirls on top of the mousse and decorate with the orange slices. Chill in the refrigerator before serving.

Chocolate Raspberry Mille Feuille

SERVES 6

450 g/1 lb puff pastry,
   thawed if frozen
1 quantity raspberry
   chocolate ganache (see
   page 278), chilled
700 g/1½ lbs fresh

raspberries, plus extra
   for decorating
icing sugar for dusting

For the raspberry sauce:
225 g/8 oz fresh raspberries

2 tbsp seedless raspberry jam
1–2 tbsp caster sugar, or
   to taste
2 tbsp lemon juice or
   framboise liqueur

Preheat the oven to 200°C/400°F/Gas Mark 6, 15 minutes before baking. Lightly oil a large baking sheet and sprinkle with a little water. Roll out the pastry on a lightly floured surface to a rectangle about 43 x 28 cm/17 x 11 inches. Cut into three long strips. Mark each strip crossways at 6.5 cm/2½ inch intervals using a sharp knife – this will make cutting the baked pastry easier and neater. Carefully transfer to the baking sheet, keeping the edges as straight as possible. Bake in the preheated oven for 20 minutes or until well risen and golden brown. Place on a wire rack and cool. Carefully transfer each rectangle to a work surface and using a sharp knife, trim the long edges straight. Cut along the knife marks to make 18 rectangles.

Place all the ingredients for the raspberry sauce in a food processor and blend until smooth. If the purée is too thick, add a little water. Taste and adjust the sweetness if necessary. Strain into a bowl, cover and chill in the refrigerator.

Place one pastry rectangle on the work surface flat-side down, spread with a little chocolate ganache and sprinkle with a few fresh raspberries. Spread a second rectangle with a little ganache, place over the first, pressing gently, then sprinkle with a few raspberries. Place a third rectangle on top, flat-side up, and spread with a little chocolate ganache. Arrange some raspberries on top and dust lightly with a little icing sugar. Repeat with the remaining pastry rectangles, chocolate ganache and fresh raspberries. Chill in the refrigerator until required and serve with the raspberry sauce and any remaining fresh raspberries.

Try this: FOR AN ALTERNATIVE: 80   FOR KIDS: 82

Chocolate & Rum Truffles

MAKES 44

For the chocolate truffles:
225 g/8 oz plain chocolate
25 g/1 oz butter, softened
2 medium egg yolks
2 tsp brandy or kirsch
2 tsp double cream

24 maraschino
   cherries, drained
2 tbsp cocoa powder, sifted

For the rum truffles:
125 g/4 oz plain

   dark chocolate
2 tbsp rum
125 ml/4 fl oz double cream
50 g/2 oz ground almonds
2 tbsp icing sugar, sifted

For the chocolate truffles, break the chocolate into pieces and place in a heatproof bowl set over a saucepan of gently simmering water. Leave for 20 minutes or until the chocolate has melted. Stir until the chocolate is smooth and remove from the heat. Leave to stand for about 6 minutes. Beat the butter, the egg yolks, the brandy or kirsch and double cream together until smooth. Stir the melted chocolate into the butter and egg yolk mixture and stir until thick. Cover and leave to cool for about 30 minutes. Chill in the refrigerator for 1½ hours or until firm.

Divide the truffle mixture into 24 pieces and mould around the drained cherries. Roll in the cocoa powder until evenly coated. Place the truffles in petit four paper cases and chill in the refrigerator for 2 hours before serving.

To make the rum truffles, break the chocolate into small pieces and place in a heavy-based saucepan with the cream and rum. Heat gently until the chocolate has melted, then stir until smooth. Stir in the ground almonds and pour into a small bowl and chill in the refrigerator for at least 6 hours or until the mixture is thick.

Remove the truffle mixture from the refrigerator and shape small spoonfuls, about the size of a cherry, into balls. Roll in the sifted icing sugar and place in petit four paper cases. Store the truffles in the refrigerator until ready to serve.

Try this: FOR AN ALTERNATIVE: 274   FOR KIDS: 280

Supreme Chocolate Gateau

CUTS INTO 10-12 SLICES

For the cake:
175 g/6 oz self-raising
    flour, sifted
1½ tsp baking powder, sifted
3 tbsp cocoa powder, sifted
175 g/6 oz margarine or

butter, softened
175 g/6 oz caster sugar
3 large eggs

To decorate:
350 g/12 oz plain

dark chocolate
1 gelatine leaf
200 ml/7 fl oz double cream
75 g/3 oz butter
cocoa powder for dusting

Preheat the oven to 180°C/350°F/Gas Mark 4, 10 minutes before baking. Line three 20.5 cm/8 inch round cake tins. Put all the cake ingredients in a bowl and whisk together until thick. Divide the mixture evenly between the prepared tins. Bake in the preheated oven for 35–40 minutes until a skewer inserted in the centre comes out clean. Cool on wire racks.

Very gently heat 2 tablespoons of hot water with 50 g/2 oz of the chocolate and stir until combined. Remove from the heat and leave for 5 minutes. Put the gelatine in a shallow dish and add 2 tablespoons of cold water. Leave for 5 minutes then squeeze out any excess water and add to the chocolate and water mixture. Stir until dissolved. Whip the double cream until just thickened. Add the chocolate mixture and continue whisking until soft peaks form. Leave until starting to set. Place one of the cakes onto a serving plate and spread with half the cream mixture. Top with a second cake and the remaining cream, cover with the third cake and chill in the refrigerator until the cream has set.

Melt 175 g/6 oz of the chocolate with the butter, stir until smooth and leave until thickened. Melt the remaining chocolate. Cut twelve 10 cm/4 inch squares of tinfoil. Spread the chocolate evenly over the squares to within 2.5 cm/1 inch of the edges. Refrigerate for 3–4 minutes until just set but not brittle. Gather up the corners and crimp together. Return to the refrigerator until firm. Spread the chocolate and butter mixture over the top and sides of the cake. Remove the foil from the curls and use to decorate. Dust with cocoa powder and serve.

Black Forest Gateau

CUTS 10-12 SLICES

250 g/9 oz butter
1 tbsp instant coffee
   granules
350 ml/12 fl oz hot water
200 g/7 oz plain dark
   chocolate, chopped

   or broken
400 g/14 oz caster sugar
225 g/8 oz self-raising flour
150 g/5 oz plain flour
50 g/2 oz cocoa powder
2 medium eggs

2 tsp vanilla essence
2 x 400 g cans stoned
   cherries in juice
2 tsp arrowroot
600 ml/1 pint double cream
50 ml/2 fl oz kirsch

Preheat the oven to 150˚C/300˚F/Gas Mark 2, 5 minutes before baking. Lightly oil and line a deep 23 cm/9 inch cake tin. Melt the butter in a large saucepan. Blend the coffee with the hot water, add to the butter with the chocolate and sugar and heat gently, stirring until smooth. Pour into a large bowl and leave until just warm.

Sift together the flours and cocoa powder. Using an electric mixer, whisk the warm chocolate mixture on a low speed, then gradually whisk in the dry ingredients. Whisk in the eggs one at a time, then the vanilla essence. Pour the mixture into the prepared tin and bake in the preheated oven for 1 hour 45 minutes or until firm and a skewer inserted into the centre comes out clean. Leave in the tin for 5 minutes to cool slightly before turning out onto a wire rack. Place the cherries and their juice in a small saucepan and heat gently. Blend the arrowroot with 2 teaspoons of water until smooth, then stir into the cherries. Cook, stirring, until the liquid thickens. Simmer very gently for 2 minutes, then leave until cold.

Whisk the double cream until thick. Trim the top of the cake if necessary, then split the cake into three layers. Brush the base of the cake with half the kirsch. Top with a layer of cream and one third of the cherries. Repeat the layering, then place the third layer on top. Reserve a little cream for decorating and use the remainder to cover the top and sides of the cake. Pipe a decorative edge around the cake, then arrange the remaining cherries in the centre and serve.

Try this: FOR AN ALTERNATIVE: 68   FOR KIDS: 342

White Chocolate & Raspberry Mousse Gateau

CUTS 8 SLICES

4 medium eggs
125 g/4 oz caster sugar
75 g/3 oz plain flour, sifted
25 g/1 oz cornflour, sifted
3 gelatine leaves
450 g/1 lb raspberries,

thawed if frozen
400 g/14 oz white chocolate
200 g/7 oz plain
   fromage frais
2 medium egg whites
25 g/1 oz caster sugar

4 tbsp raspberry or
   orange liqueur
200 ml/7 fl oz double cream
fresh raspberries, halved,
   to decorate

Preheat the oven to 190°C/375°F/Gas Mark 5, 10 minutes before baking. Oil and line two 23 cm/9 inch cake tins. Whisk the eggs and sugar until thick and creamy and the whisk leaves a trail in the mixture. Fold in the flour and cornflour, then divide between the tins. Bake in the preheated oven for 12–15 minutes or until risen and firm. Cool in the tins, then turn out onto wire racks. Place the gelatine with 4 tablespoons of cold water in a dish and leave to soften for 5 minutes. Purée half the raspberries, press through a sieve, then heat until nearly boiling. Squeeze out excess water from the gelatine, add to the purée and stir until dissolved.

Melt 175 g/6 oz of the chocolate in a bowl set over a saucepan of simmering water. Leave to cool, then stir in the fromage frais and purée. Whisk the egg whites until stiff and whisk in the sugar. Fold into the raspberry mixture with the rest of the raspberries. Line the sides of a 23 cm/9 inch springform tin with non-stick baking parchment. Place one layer of sponge in the base and sprinkle with half the liqueur. Pour in the raspberry mixture and top with the second sponge. Brush with the remaining liqueur. Press down and chill in the refrigerator for 4 hours. Unmould onto a plate.

Cut a strip of double thickness non-stick baking paper to fit around the cake and stand 1 cm/½ inch higher. Melt the remaining white chocolate and spread thickly onto the paper. Leave until just setting. Wrap around the cake and freeze for 15 minutes. Peel away the paper. Whip the cream until thick and spread over the top. Decorate with raspberries and serve.

Try this: FOR AN ALTERNATIVE: 320   FOR KIDS: 258

Chocolate & Almond Daquoise with Summer Berries

CUTS INTO 8 SERVINGS

For the almond meringues:
6 large egg whites
¼ tsp cream of tartar
275 g/10 oz caster sugar
½ tsp almond essence
50 g/2 oz blanched or flaked
 almonds, lightly toasted
 and finely ground

**For the chocolate
 buttercream:**
75 g/3 oz butter, softened
450 g/1 lb icing sugar, sifted
50 g/2 oz cocoa
 powder, sifted
3–4 tbsp milk or
 single cream

550 g/1¼ lb mixed summer
 berries such as
 raspberries, strawberries
 and blackberries

To decorate:
toasted flaked almonds
icing sugar

Preheat the oven to 140°C/275°F/Gas Mark 1, 10 minutes before baking. Line three baking sheets with non-stick baking paper and draw a 20.5 cm/8 inch round on each one.

Whisk the egg whites and cream of tartar until soft peaks form. Gradually beat in the sugar, 2 tablespoons at a time, beating well after each addition, until the whites are stiff and glossy. Beat in the almond essence, then using a metal spoon or rubber spatula gently fold in the ground almonds.

Divide the mixture evenly between the three circles of baking paper, spreading neatly into the rounds and smoothing the tops evenly. Bake in the preheated oven for about 1¼ hours or until crisp, rotating the baking sheets halfway through cooking. Turn off the oven, allow to cool for about 1 hour, then remove and cool completely before discarding the lining paper

Beat the butter, icing sugar and cocoa powder until smooth and creamy, adding the milk or cream to form a soft consistency. Reserve about a quarter of the berries to decorate. Spread one meringue with a third of the buttercream and top with a third of the remaining berries. Repeat with the other meringue rounds, buttercream and berries. Scatter with the toasted flaked almonds, the reserved berries and sprinkle with icing sugar and serve.

Try this: FOR AN ALTERNATIVE: 292 FOR KIDS: 272

Chocolate Mousse Cake

CUTS INTO 8-10 SERVINGS

For the cake:
450 g/1 lb plain dark
    chocolate, chopped
125 g/4 oz butter, softened
3 tbsp brandy
9 large eggs, separated

150 g/5 oz caster sugar

For the chocolate glaze:
225 ml/8 fl oz double cream
225 g/8 oz plain dark
    chocolate, chopped

2 tbsp brandy
1 tbsp single cream and
    white chocolate curls,
    to decorate

Preheat the oven to 180°C/350°F/Gas Mark 4, 10 minutes before baking. Line the bases of two 20.5 cm/8 inch springform tins with baking paper. Melt the chocolate and butter in a bowl set over a saucepan of simmering water. Stir until smooth. Remove from the heat and stir in the brandy. Whisk the egg yolks and the sugar, reserving 2 tablespoons of the sugar, until thick and creamy. Slowly beat in the chocolate mixture until smooth and well blended. Whisk the egg whites until soft peaks form, then sprinkle over the remaining sugar and continue whisking until stiff but not dry.

Fold a large spoonful of the egg whites into the chocolate mixture. Gently fold in the remaining egg whites. Divide about two thirds of the mixture evenly between the tins, tapping to distribute the mixture evenly. Reserve the remaining chocolate mousse mixture for the filling. Bake in the preheated oven for about 20 minutes, or until the cakes are well risen and set. Remove and cool for at least 1 hour. Loosen the edges of the cake layers with a knife. Using your fingertips, lightly press the crusty edges down. Pour the rest of the mousse over one layer, spreading until even. Unclip the side, remove the other cake from the tin and gently invert on to the mousse, bottom side up to make a flat top layer. Discard the lining paper and chill for 4–6 hours, or until set.

To make the glaze, melt the cream and chocolate with the brandy in a heavy-based saucepan and stir until smooth. Cool until thickened. Unclip the side of the mousse cake and place on a wire rack. Pour over half the glaze and spread to cover. Allow to set, then decorate with chocolate curls. To serve, heat the remaining glaze and pour round each slice, and dot with cream.

Chocolate Box Cake

CUTS INTO 16 SLICES

For the chocolate sponge:
175 g/6 oz self-raising flour
1 tsp baking powder
175 g/6 oz caster sugar
175 g/6 oz butter, softened
3 large eggs
25 g/1 oz cocoa powder

150 g/5 oz apricot preserve
cocoa powder, to dust

For the chocolate box:
275 g/10 oz plain dark
   chocolate

For the chocolate topping:
450 ml ¾ pint double cream
275 g/10 oz plain dark
   chocolate, melted
2 tbsp brandy
1 tsp cocoa powder,
   to decorate

Preheat the oven to 180°C/350°F/Gas Mark 4, 10 minutes before baking. Lightly oil and flour a 20.5 cm/8 inch square cake tin. Sift the flour and baking powder into a large bowl and stir in the sugar. Using an electric whisk, beat in the butter and eggs. Blend the cocoa powder with 1 tablespoon of water, then beat into the creamed mixture. Turn into the tin and bake in the preheated oven for about 25 minutes, or until well risen and cooked. Remove and cool before removing the cake from the tin.

To make the chocolate box, break the chocolate into small pieces, place in a heatproof bowl over a saucepan of gently simmering water and leave until soft. Stir it occasionally until melted and smooth. Line a Swiss roll tin with non-stick baking paper then pour in the melted chocolate, tilting the tin to level. Leave until set. Once the chocolate is set, turn out on to a chopping board and carefully strip off the paper. Cut into four strips, the same length as the cooked sponge, using a large sharp knife that has been dipped into hot water. Gently heat the apricot preserve and sieve to remove lumps. Brush over the top and sides of the cake. Carefully place the chocolate strips around the cake sides and press lightly. Leave to set for at least 10 minutes.

For the topping, whisk the cream to soft peaks and quickly fold into the melted chocolate with the brandy. Spoon the chocolate whipped cream into a pastry bag fitted with a star nozzle and pipe a decorative design over the surface. Dust with cocoa power and serve.

Try this: FOR AN ALTERNATIVE: 198   FOR KIDS: 230

Grated Chocolate Roulade

CUTS 8 SLICES

4 medium eggs, separated
125 g/4 oz caster sugar
60 g/2½ oz plain dark
  chocolate, grated

75 g/3 oz self-raising
  flour, sifted
2 tbsp caster sugar, plus
  extra for sprinkling

150 ml/¼ pint double cream
2 tsp icing sugar
1 tsp vanilla essence
chocolate curls, to decorate

Preheat the oven to 180°C/350°F/Gas Mark 4, 10 minutes before serving. Lightly oil and line a 20.5 x 30.5 cm/8 x 12 inch Swiss roll tin. Beat the egg yolks and sugar with an electric mixer for 5 minutes or until thick, then stir in 2 tablespoons of hot water and the grated chocolate. Finally fold in the sifted flour.

Whisk the egg whites until stiff, then fold 1–2 tablespoons of egg white into the chocolate mixture. Mix lightly, then gently fold in the remaining egg white. Pour into the prepared tin and bake in the preheated oven for about 12 minutes or until firm.

Place a large sheet of non-stick baking parchment on to a work surface and sprinkle liberally with caster sugar. Turn the cake onto the baking parchment, discard the lining paper and trim away the crisp edges. Roll up as for a Swiss roll cake, leave for 2 minutes, then unroll and leave to cool.

Beat the double cream with the icing sugar and vanilla essence until thick. Reserve a little for decoration, then spread the remaining cream over the cake, leaving a 2.5 cm/1 inch border all round. Using the greaseproof paper, roll up from a short end.

Carefully transfer the roulade to a large serving plate and use the reserved cream to decorate the top. Add the chocolate curls just before serving, then cut into slices and serve. Store in the refrigerator

Try this: FOR AN ALTERNATIVE: 74 FOR KIDS: 84

Chocolate Hazelnut Meringue Gateau

CUTS INTO 8-10 SLICES

5 medium egg whites
275 g/10 oz caster sugar
125 g/4 oz hazelnuts, toasted
and finely chopped
175 g/6 oz plain

dark chocolate
100 g/3½ oz butter
3 medium eggs, separated
plus 1 medium egg white
25 g/1 oz icing sugar

125 ml/4 fl oz double cream
hazelnuts, toasted and
chopped, to decorate

Preheat the oven to 150°C/300°F/Gas Mark 2, 5 minutes before baking. Cut three pieces of non-stick baking parchment into 30.5 x 12.5 cm/12 x 5 inch rectangles and then place onto two or three baking sheets.

Whisk the egg whites until stiff, add half the sugar and whisk until the mixture is stiff, smooth and glossy. Whisk in the remaining sugar, 1 tablespoon at a time, beating well between each addition. When all the sugar has been added whisk for 1 minute. Stir in the hazelnuts. Spoon the meringue inside the marked rectangles spreading in a continuous backwards and forwards movement. Bake in the preheated oven for 1¼ hours, remove and leave until cold. Trim the meringues until they measure 25.5 x 10 cm/10 x 4 inches. Reserve all the trimmings.

Melt the chocolate and the butter in a heatproof bowl set over a saucepan of gently simmering water and stir until smooth. Remove from the heat and beat in the egg yolks. Whisk the egg whites until stiff, then whisk in the icing sugar a little at a time. Fold the egg whites into the chocolate mixture and chill in the refrigerator for 20–30 minutes, until thick enough to spread. Whip the double cream until soft peaks form. Reserve.

Place one of the meringue layers onto a serving plate. Spread with about half of the mousse mixture, then top with a second meringue layer. Spread the remaining mouse mixture over the top with the third meringue. Spread the cream over the top and sprinkle with the chopped hazelnuts. Chill in the refrigerator for at least 4 hours. Serve cut into slices.

Try this: FOR AN ALTERNATIVE: 80 FOR KIDS: 292

Christmas Cranberry Chocolate Roulade

CUTS INTO 12-14 SLICES

For the granache frosting:
300 ml/½ pint double cream
350 g/12 oz plain dark
   chocolate, chopped
2 tbsp brandy (optional)

For the roulade:
5 large eggs, separated

3 tbsp cocoa powder, sifted,
   plus extra for dusting
125 g/4 oz icing sugar, sifted,
   plus extra for dusting
¼ tsp cream of tartar

For the filling:
175 g/6 oz cranberry sauce

1–2 tbsp brandy (optional)
450 ml/¾ pint double cream,
   whipped to soft peaks

To decorate:
caramelised orange strips
dried cranberries

Preheat the oven to 200°C /400°F/Gas Mark 6. Bring the cream to the boil over a medium heat. Remove from the heat and add all of the chocolate, stirring until melted. Stir in the brandy, if using and strain into a medium bowl. Cool, then refrigerate for 6–8 hours.

Line a 39 x 26 cm/15½ x 10½ inch Swiss roll tin with non-stick baking paper. Using an electric whisk, beat the egg yolks until thick and creamy. Slowly beat in the cocoa powder and half the icing sugar and reserve. Whisk the egg whites and cream of tartar into soft peaks. Gradually whisk in the remaining sugar until the mixture is stiff and glossy. Gently fold the yolk mixture into the egg whites with a metal spoon. Spread evenly into the tin. Bake in the preheated oven for 15 minutes. Remove and invert on to a large sheet of greaseproof paper, dusted with cocoa powder. Cut off the crisp edges of the cake then roll up. Leave on a wire rack until cold.

For the filling, heat the cranberry sauce with the brandy, if using, until warm and spreadable. Unroll the cooled cake and spread with the cranberry sauce. Allow to cool and set. Carefully spoon the whipped cream over the surface and spread to within 2.5 cm/1 inch of the edges. Re-roll the cake. Transfer to a cake plate or tray. Allow the chocolate ganache to soften at room temperature, then beat until soft and of a spreadable consistency. Spread over the roulade and dust with icing sugar. Decorate with the orange strips and cranberries and serve.

Try this: FOR AN ALTERNATIVE: 336 FOR KIDS: 106

Peach & White Chocolate Gateau

CUTS INTO 8-10 SLICES

175 g/6 oz unsalted
  butter, softened
2 tsp grated orange rind
175 g/6 oz caster sugar
3 medium eggs
100 g/3½ oz white chocolate,
  melted and cooled

225 g/8 oz self-raising
  flour, sifted
300 ml/½ pint double cream
40 g/1½ oz icing sugar
125 g/4 oz hazelnuts, toasted
  and chopped

For the peach filling:
2 ripe peaches, peeled and
  chopped
2 tbsp peach or orange
  liqueur
300 ml/½ pint double cream
40 g/1½ oz icing sugar

Preheat the oven to 170°C/325°F/Gas Mark 3, 10 minutes before baking. Lightly oil and line a deep 23 cm/9 inch round cake tin. Cream the butter, orange rind and sugar together until light and fluffy. Add the eggs, one at a time, beating well after each addition, then beat in the cooled white chocolate. Add the flour and 175 ml/6 fl oz of water in two batches. Spoon into the prepared tin and bake in the preheated oven for 1½ hours or until firm. Leave to stand for at least 5 minutes before turning out onto a wire rack to cool completely.

To make the filling, place the peaches in a bowl and pour over the liqueur. Leave to stand for 30 minutes. Whip the cream with the icing sugar until soft peaks form, then fold in the peach mixture. Split the cold cake in to three layers, place one layer on a serving plate and spread with half the peach filling. Top with a second sponge layer and spread with the remaining peach filling. Top with the remaining cake.

Whip the cream and icing sugar together until soft peaks form. Spread over the top and sides of the cake, piping some onto the top if liked. Press the hazelnuts into the side of cake and if liked sprinkle a few on top. Chill in the refrigerator until required. Serve cut into slices. Store the cake in the refrigerator.

Chocolate Fudge Sundae

SERVES 2

For the chocolate
fudge sauce:
75 g/3 oz plain dark
chocolate, broken
into pieces
450ml/¾ pint double cream
175g/6 oz golden
caster sugar

25 g/1 oz plain flour
pinch of salt
15 g/½ oz unsalted butter
1 tsp vanilla essence

For the sundae:
125 g/4 oz raspberries, fresh
or thawed if frozen

4 scoops vanilla ice cream
2 scoops chocolate
ice cream
2 tbsp toasted flaked
almonds
a few wafers,
to serve

To make the chocolate fudge sauce, place the chocolate and cream in a heavy-based saucepan and heat gently until the chocolate has melted into the cream. Stir until smooth. Mix the sugar with the flour and salt, then stir in sufficient chocolate mixture to make a smooth paste.

Gradually blend the remaining melted chocolate mixture into the paste, then pour into a clean saucepan. Cook over a low heat, stirring frequently until smooth and thick. Remove from the heat and add the butter and vanilla essence. Stir until smooth, then cool slightly.

To make the sundae, crush the raspberries lightly with a fork and reserve. Spoon a little of the chocolate sauce into the bottom of two sundae glasses. Add a layer of crushed raspberries, then a scoop each of vanilla and chocolate ice cream.

Top each one with a scoop of the vanilla ice cream. Pour over the sauce, sprinkle over the almonds and serve with a wafer.

Try this: FOR AN ALTERNATIVE: 322 FOR KIDS: 348

Black & White Torte

CUTS INTO 8-10 SLICES

4 medium eggs
150 g/5 oz caster sugar
50 g/2 oz cornflour
50 g/2 oz plain flour
50 g/2 oz self-raising flour

900 ml/1½ pints double cream
150 g/5 oz plain dark
    chocolate, chopped
300 g/11 oz white
    chocolate, chopped

6 tbsp Grand Marnier, or
    other orange liqueur
cocoa powder for dusting

Preheat the oven to 180°C/350°F/Gas Mark 4, 10 minutes before baking. Line a 23 cm/ 9 inch round cake tin. Beat the eggs and sugar in a large bowl until thick and creamy. Sift together the cornflour, plain flour and self-raising flour three times, then lightly fold into the egg mixture. Spoon the mixture into the prepared tin and bake in the preheated oven for 35–40 minutes or until firm. Turn the cake out onto a wire rack and leave to cool.

Place 300 ml/½ pint of the double cream in a saucepan and bring to the boil. Immediately remove from the heat and add the plain chocolate and a further tablespoon of the liqueur. Stir until smooth. Repeat using the remaining cream, white chocolate and liqueur. Chill in the refrigerator for 2 hours, then whisk each mixture until thick and creamy.

Place the dark chocolate mixture in a piping bag fitted with a plain nozzle and place half the white chocolate mixture in a separate piping bag fitted with a plain nozzle. Reserve the remaining white chocolate mixture.

Split the cold cake horizontally into two layers. Brush or drizzle the remaining liqueur over the cakes. Put one layer onto a serving plate. Pipe alternating rings of white and dark chocolate mixture to cover the first layer of cake. Use the reserved white chocolate mixture to cover the top and sides of the cake. Dust with cocoa powder, cut into slices and serve. Store in the refrigerator.

Try this: FOR AN ALTERNATIVE: 76 FOR KIDS: 68

Chocolate Chip Ice Cream

SERVES 4

350 g/12 oz fresh raspberries, or thawed if frozen
25 g/1 oz icing sugar, or to taste
2 tbsp lemon juice

600 ml/1 pint milk
1 vanilla pod, seeds removed
6 medium egg yolks
125 g/4 oz caster sugar

450 g/1 lb plain dark chocolate
150 ml/¼ pint double cream
fresh fruit of your choice, to serve

Set the freezer to rapid freeze. Simmer the raspberries with the sugar and lemon juice for 5 minutes. Leave to cool, then purée in a food processor. Press through a fine sieve to remove the pips. Reserve the coulis.

Pour the milk into a heavy-based saucepan and add the vanilla pod. Bring slowly to the boil, then remove from the heat and leave to infuse for 30 minutes. Remove the pod. Whisk the egg yolks and caster sugar together until pale and creamy, then gradually whisk in the infused milk. Strain the mixture into a clean saucepan, place over a gentle heat and bring slowly to the boil. Cook over a gentle heat, stirring constantly, until the mixture thickens and coats the back of a wooden spoon. Do not let the mixture boil otherwise it will curdle. Once thickened, cover with clingfilm and leave the custard to cool completely.

Break half the chocolate into small pieces and place in a heatproof bowl set over a saucepan of gently simmering water. Heat gently, stirring frequently, until the chocolate has melted and smooth. Remove from the heat and leave to cool. Whip the cream until soft peaks form and fold into the cooled custard. Roughly chop the remaining chocolate and stir into the custard mixture together with the melted chocolate. Spoon into a suitable container and freeze for 1 hour. Remove from the freezer and beat well to break up all the ice crystals. Repeat the beating and freezing process twice more, then freeze for 4 hours or until the ice cream is solid. Allow to soften in the refrigerator for 30 minutes before serving with fresh fruit and the raspberry coulis. Remember to return the freezer to its normal setting.

Try this: FOR AN ALTERNATIVE: 288   FOR KIDS: 344

Index